Arizona Bucket List Adventure Guide

Explore 100 Offbeat Destinations You Must Visit!

Michael Cordova

Canyon Press
canyon@purplelink.org

Please consider writing a review!
Just visit: purplelink.org/review

ISBN: 978-1-957590-01-1

FREE BONUS

Discover 31 Incredible Places You Can
Visit Next. Just Go To:

purplelink.org/travel

Table of Contents:

How to Use This Book

Welcome to your very own adventure guide to exploring the many wonders of the state of Arizona. Not only does this book offer the most wonderful places to visit and sights to see in the vast state, but it provides GPS coordinates for Google Maps to make exploring that much easier.

Adventure Guide

Sorted by region, this guide offers over 100 amazing wonders found in Arizona for you to see and explore. They can be visited in any order, and this book will help you keep track of where you've been and where to look forward to going next. Each section describes the area or place, what to look for, how to get there, and what you may need to bring along.

GPS Coordinates

As you can imagine, not all of the locations in this book have a physical address. Fortunately, some of our listed wonders are either located within a National Park or Reserve or near a city, town, or place of business. For those that are not associated with a specific location, it is easiest to map it using GPS coordinates.

Luckily, Google has a system of codes that converts the coordinates into pin-drop locations that Google Maps can interpret and navigate.

Each adventure in this guide includes GPS coordinates along with a physical address whenever it is available.

It is important that you are prepared for poor cell signals. It is recommended that you route your location and ensure that the directions are accessible offline. Depending on your device and the distance of some locations, you may need to travel with a backup battery source.

About Arizona

Arizona was the 48th state admitted to the United States, and its unique natural landscape, with locations such as the Grand Canyon, Monument Valley, and Havasu Falls, has been a staple of the area's history. Its major cities, Phoenix, Tucson, and Scottsdale offer "home bases" for those wanting to explore the wonders of the state.

Before statehood, Arizona was home to Native Americans for thousands of years. The Navajo and Tohono O'odham Nations are currently the two largest reservations in the United States. The history and influence of the region's indigenous people can be seen around the state, with historical landmarks that allow for further education. The Mesa Verde are some of the best-preserved pueblos (villages) in North America. Created nearly a millennium ago, around 1190, these homes provide insight into the Pueblo people's world.

The Colorado River's power has been the life force of the state for nearly 70 million years. Carving out the landscape of the northern region, including the famed Grand Canyon, the river's strength even supplies the surrounding states with water and power due to the Hoover Dam. The dam also protects Arizona, California, and Nevada from potential flooding during a rise in the Colorado River.

The rich history of Arizona and its unique landscape has brought visitors to the region for hundreds of years. With the continued support of the national parks, these protected regions can be enjoyed for many more years.

Landscape and Climate

The state has multiple landscapes and climates, with the north and south regions being nearly opposite to one another. Each region has its own plants and animals that call the area home and have been there for hundreds of years. There are three geographical regions of Arizona: The Basin and Range (south), Transition Zone (middle), and Colorado Plateau (north).

The southern region of the state has a desert climate within the Basin and Range region. There is extreme heat in summers, many days with temperatures above 100°F (37.8°C), and mild temperatures in the winter around 50°F (10°C). This region of the state receives little rainfall during the year, furthering the intense climate. Many of the native plants are cacti. Among the vast number in the region, some flower while others grow multiple feet tall.

The Colorado Plateau that encompasses the northern region of the state, has a less extreme climate, allowing for the growth of pine tree forests. The largest ponderosa pine trees in the world are located in Arizona. With the Colorado Plateau running across the region, mountains and canyons have formed in the areas. During the winter, this region experiences nearly 40 inches of snow in some areas, allowing ski resorts to operate. The Colorado River runs through the northwest area of the state and formed the Grand Canyon. The Hoover Dam is located on the border of Arizona and Nevada.

The state's two major geographic regions offer two vastly different landscapes and climates within a small area. Visitors to the state can experience different scenic experiences without needing to travel far.

4

Organ Pipe Cactus National Monument

Located in the very south of Arizona, only miles from the Mexican border, the Organ Pipe Cactus National Monument was declared an International Biosphere (UNESCO) reserve in 1977. In 1937, the land was donated by the state of Arizona and made into a national monument. The protection of the area has allowed for plants and animals to thrive. The region contains 517 square miles and is the only place in the United States where senita and organ pipe cacti grow. This region of organ pipe cactus has been dated to the Sonoran Desert around 3,500 years ago. These cacti can live up to 150 years; it takes 35 years before they produce flowers. The cacti's flowers are only open at night toward mid-morning in May and June. There are two scenic drives through the monument. The Ajo drive is the most popular and, with 21 miles of road, it is also the most popular biking trail. The Puerto Blanco drive is made up of two sections, North and South. The loop is 41 miles in total and takes around three to five hours to drive round trip.

Best Time to Visit: October to June

Pass/Permit/Fees: $12 per car

Closest City or Town: Ajo

Physical Address: Kris Eggle Visitor Center, 10 Organ Pipe Dr, Ajo, AZ 85321

GPS Coordinates: 32.0878° N, 112.9059° W

Did You Know? These cacti get their name from the many stems (or arms) that grow off the cactus.

Apache-Sitgreaves National Forests

Located in eastern Arizona, the Apache-Sitgreaves National Forests cover over two million acres of land. The Sitgreaves Forest was named after Captain Sitgreaves, who conducted scientific expeditions in the area in the 1850s, while the Apache Forest was named for the Native American tribes that lived in the region. With over 400 different species of wildlife, there are four wilderness areas in the park to educate visitors.

There are over 1,000 miles of trails for hiking, horseback riding, or biking. The two forests contain 34 lakes and reservoirs and more than 680 miles of rivers and streams, making them one of the top locations for fishing in the country. Throughout the woods, there are remains of pueblos (villages), showcasing carved and painted images on the walls dating over 60 to 900 years old. Some of the oldest wall paintings can be seen at the Blue Crossing Campground.

Best Time to Visit: March to May; October to November

Pass/Permit/Fees: Free

Closest City or Town: Alpine

Physical Address: Blue Crossing Campground, US 180, Forest Route 281, Alpine, AZ 85920

GPS Coordinates: 34.3885° N, 110.6170° W

Did You Know? One chipmunk in the Apache-Sitgreaves forest can gather 165 acorns in one day.

Pacheta Falls

Located in the Grand White Mountains, the Pacheta Falls are much less crowded than others in the state, making it popular among hikers who enjoy a quiet and more secluded hike. The waterfall is surrounded by rock formations and lush green vegetation. The falls stand over 131 feet high and are surrounded by Douglas fir trees, a sharp contrast to Arizona's typical desert climate. Unfortunately, swimming is not allowed at these falls because the rocks and water current make it too dangerous. The hike to reach the falls is only 2.5 miles round trip, although a much longer car ride is needed to get to the trailhead – about two hours.

Because the falls are isolated, it's very common to see wildlife, including elk, bears, and bighorn sheep. The falls are located on the White Mountain Apache Reservation, and a special permit is required to enter the area. West of the falls is the meeting point of the three creeks: the Spud, Ess, and Pacheta Creeks (which feeds the Pacheta Falls).

Best Time to Visit: March to October

Pass/Permit/Fees: Black River Special Use Permit, $15

Closest City or Town: Alpine

Physical Address: Pacheta Falls, Co Rd 70, Whiteriver, AZ 85941

GPS Coordinates: 33.6674° N, 109.5249° W

Did You Know? This is one of the largest waterfalls and the most secluded in Arizona.

Superstition Mountain Museum

Located in the foothills of Superstition Mountain, with huge red rocks towering behind, is the Superstition Mountain Museum. The museum was created by several members who founded the Superstition Mountain Historical Society, Inc. in 1980. The museum and historical society were established to preserve the history of Jacob Waltz and the Lost Dutchman Mine. The legend claims that $200 million in treasure is hidden in the mountain, and many hunters have died trying to find it. The mountain is full of pre-Columbian and Native American lore and legends that are also being preserved for future generations.

The museum includes outdoor structures, among them a 20-stamp gold mill, an Elvis Chapel, a mountain man camp, Western storefronts, and a labeled Nature Walk.

Best Time to Visit: March to May

Pass/Permit/Fees: $5 per adult

Closest City or Town: Apache Junction

Physical Address: Superstition Mountain Museum, 4087 E Apache Trail, Apache Junction, AZ 85119

GPS Coordinates: 33.4471° N, 111.5017° W

Did You Know? TV shows have filmed at Superstition Mountain, trying to find the Lost Dutchman Mine and hidden treasure.

Kartchner Caverns

Two people who were exploring the limestone hills in the Whetstone Mountains discovered these caverns in 1974 but kept it a secret until 1978. The limestone caverns are filled with speleothem, a mineral deposit that is common in caves, forming typical stalagmites. Inside Kartchner Cavern, the speleothem has been growing for over 50,000 years, and precautions have been taken to protect it.

The Kartchner Cavern is considered a "living" cave because the formations within are still growing. The "World's Largest Soda Straw" stalactites, measuring at 21 feet, are in the Throne Room. The Big Room features the world's most extensive formation of brushite moonmilk. During the summer months, a colony of over 2,000 cave bats uses it as a nursery roost.

Best Time to Visit: Year-round, but some of the cave is closed in the summer due to bats

Pass/Permit/Fees: $7 per vehicle, and tours of the cave cost additional fees

Closest City or Town: Benson

Physical Address: Kartchner Caverns, 2980 AZ-90, Benson, AZ 85602

GPS Coordinates: 31.8366° N, 110.3489° W

Did You Know? Over 60% of the cave system is not open to the public.

Bisbee

In 1877, U.S. Army scouts and cavalrymen were sent into Arizona to search the area for Apaches. Jack Dunn found signs of minerals (lead, copper, and silver) and decided to settle the region. The town was founded in 1880 and named after Judge DeWitt Bisbee, one of the financial backers of the Copper Queen Mine. The area's open-pit mines became very busy because of the demand for copper during World War I. By the 1950s, most of the mines had closed down, and the town's population declined considerably. The Bisbee mayor decided to turn a section of the Copper Queen Mine into an attraction to increase tourism and improve the region's economy. Volunteers cleared fallen rock and re-timbered the mine to create the sections for visitors.

The historic city, "Old Bisbee," is full of Victorian-style houses and an Art Deco county courthouse. Bisbee is a prime example of a mining town and the growth the region has experienced since the ending of mining.

Best Time to Visit: March to June

Pass/Permit/Fees: None

Closest City or Town: Bisbee

Physical Address: Copper Queen Plaza, 2 Main St, Bisbee, AZ 85603

GPS Coordinates: 31.4420° N, 109.9151° W

Did You Know? The old high school has four floors, each with its own ground-level entrance due to the hilly terrain.

10

Copper Queen Mine

Located in Bisbee, Arizona, the Copper Queen Mine operated for nearly 100 years and produced $6.1 billion in 1975 currency, which would be $30.8 billion in modern-day currency. There are over 2,000 miles of tunnels in the mine, making it one of the largest in the world. During its peak mining era, more than eight billion pounds of copper were found. After the decline of mining and the economy in Bisbee, officials decided to open the mines for tours with the help of volunteers. The old mines were cleared of rock, and the workways were re-timbered. The mine is no longer active and is now used for tours to educate and show what mining in the American Southwest was like during that time. There is still evidence of mining at the site, including tools, a desk, and carts. Visitors wear hardhats and miner's headlamps and travel 1,500 feet into the mine; many of the tour guides have worked in the mines and offer their personal stories.

Best Time to Visit: Year-round

Pass/Permit/Fees: $13 adults, $5 children

Closest City or Town: Bisbee

Physical Address: Copper Queen Mine Tours, 478 N Dart Rd, Bisbee, AZ 85603

GPS Coordinates: 34.4556° N, 112.1935° W

Did You Know? The mine produced 8,032,352,000 pounds of copper, 2,871,786 ounces of gold, 77,162,986 ounces of silver, 304,627,600 pounds of lead and 371,945,900 pounds of zinc.

"The Goon" World War II Memorial

On your way to the Queen Mine Tour in Bisbee, stop at the Lavender Pit, featuring the WWII memorial for the famed B-24 fighter jet shot down over Hong Kong in 1943. Arthur Benko, a Bisbee native, was the gunner aboard "The Goon" as it went down. The soldiers were able to survive the crash by tossing everything off the plane, and the pilot landed it safely on base in Kweilin, China. Benko and another soldier, Lt. Malcolm S. Sanders, were later killed in action. The remaining eight soldiers, including the pilot, survived. The memorial is dedicated to Benko and the 76 other men from Bisbee who served in WWII.

Behind The Goon is the Lavender Pit, an open-pit copper mine that spans 300 acres and is 900 feet deep. It produced 86 million tons of copper, gold, and silver ore until it shut down in 1974. Lavender Pit is smaller than the Queen Mine but steeper than other open-pit mines of the time.

Best Time to Visit: Year-Round

Pass/Permit/Fees: Free to see

Closest City or Town: Bisbee

Physical Address: Lavender Pit, AZ-80 E, Bisbee, Arizona 85603

GPS Coordinates: 31.4355° N, 109.9026° W

Did You Know? Arthur J. Benko is the Top Gunner in the U.S. Air Force with a confirmed 16 kills and was posthumously awarded the Silver Star.

Tombstone

Tombstone is a historic city founded in 1877 by prospector Ed Schieffelin. It is most famous for the "Gunfight at the OK Corral," one of the best-known shootouts in the American Wild West. By 1881, the city was thriving and had restaurants, four churches, and even Vogan's Bowling Alley. While the town's population decreased because of economic decline, it did remain the county's center. The Cochise County Courthouse and gallows yard are preserved here. The city was declared a National Historic Landmark District in 1961.

There are eight museums in Tombstone: the Audie Murphy & Medal of Honor Museum, the Bird Cage Theatre, Boothill Graveyard, the Gunfighter Hall of Fame, the Rose Tree Inn Museum, Tombstone Courthouse State Historic Park, the Tombstone Epitaph Museum, and the Tombstone Western Heritage Museum, which features Wyatt Earp memorabilia and items from the other Earp brothers and the Cochise County Cow-Boys.

Best Time to Visit: March to May

Pass/Permit/Fees: Free

Closest City or Town: Bisbee

Physical Address: O.K. Corral, 326 E Allen St, Tombstone, AZ 85638

GPS Coordinates: 31.7129° N, 110.0676° W

Did You Know? When Tombstone had operating mines, over 6,000 men worked in them.

Swansea Ghost Town

Swansea was originally settled in 1862 as a mining town, and the population grew when the Arizona & California Railroad began construction in 1904. By 1909, Swansea had a post office, and it was one of the few towns in the Arizona territory at the time to feature a car dealership and an electric light company. The town's smelts and mines prospered during WWI, but with declining copper prices and without an easy way to get water into Swansea, the town was entirely abandoned by 1937.

Today, Swansea is one of the most well-preserved ghost towns in the country. The Bureau of Land Management took over the land and works to restore what's left of the buildings and copper mine and installed an interpretative trail to educate visitors about the history of Swansea. Visitors claim it to be one of the creepiest ghost towns in Arizona because of the two cemeteries there.

Best Time to Visit: Year-Round

Pass/Permit/Fees: Free to visit

Closest City or Town: Bouse

Physical Address: The town is remote and can only be accessed by dirt roads. Refer to the GPS coordinates to navigate.

GPS Coordinates: 34.0514° N, 114.0668° W

Did You Know? Scenes from the 1971 crime thriller *The Day of the Wolves* were filmed in Swansea.

Montezuma Castle National Monument

Established in 1906, this was the third national monument created to protect Native American culture. It includes some of the best-preserved dwellings created by the Sinagua people, a pre-Columbian culture. The main structure is five stories high and contains 20 rooms. It was created over a period of 300 years and was misnamed when Europeans arrived, calling it Montezuma after the Aztec empire. The settlers saw the dwelling in the rock face and assumed it was used as a castle – also a mistake.

The cave buildings show that the Sinagua people were skilled builders and engineers. A series of portable ladders connected the floors, acting as a vertical barrier to prevent enemies from accessing the other levels. In addition to the dwelling, 860 acres of surrounding land are protected as part of the national monument.

Best Time to Visit: February to May

Pass/Permit/Fees: $10 per adult

Closest City or Town: Camp Verde

Physical Address: Montezuma Castle National Monument Visitor Center, 2800 Montezuma Castle Rd, Camp Verde, AZ 86322

GPS Coordinates: 34.6116° N, 111.8350° W

Did You Know? The Montezuma Castle sits 90 feet up on a sheer limestone cliff.

Canyon de Chelly

Canyon de Chelly covers 83,840 acres of land and houses three major canyons: de Chelly, del Muerto, and Monument. The canyons were formed by thousands of years of streams cutting through the region. Some of the most popular geological features are Spider Rock, Mummy Cave, and Antelope House Overlook. Before it was a national monument, the region was home to the Navajo people. The entire Canyon de Chelly region is currently owned by the Navajo Tribal Trust. This is the only national park that is owned and managed by a trust. The park still has evidence of the original people from the region in the White and Antelope House Ruins. Many of the ruins sit 600 feet off the cliffs and have over 70 rooms. These historical locations showcase carved and drawn images. The canyon has two main roads: the South Rim and the North Rim. Both roads offer scenic overlooks of Canyon de Chelly. A seasonal stream forms after snow and rain during the winter, and the Chinle Wash will form at the lower end of the canyon floor.

Best Time to Visit: April to May; September to October

Pass/Permit/Fees: Free

Closest City or Town: Chinle

Physical Address: Canyon de Chelly Welcome Center, Indian Route 7, Chinle, AZ 86503

GPS Coordinates: 36.1336° N, 109.4694° W

Did You Know? Members of the Navajo Nation still live in Canyon de Chelly.

Spider Rock in Canyon de Chelly

Spider Rock is a 750-foot sandstone spire sacred to the Navajo and Hopi people. According to Navajo legend, Spider Grandmother resides on the larger of the two spires, and her helpers, the crows, live on the shorter spire. Spider Grandmother, who takes the form of either a timeless woman or a common spider, worked with Tawa (the Sun God) to give souls to animals. After this, they made humans after their likeness and sang them to life. Spider Grandmother taught men and women their roles and religious practices before dividing them into four groups and leading them to live in the Four Canyons.

Since Spider Rock is considered a sacred location, visitors are prohibited. Its tower is visible from the South Rim Drive.

Best Time to Visit: April to May; September to October

Pass/Permit/Fees: No entrance fees

Closest City or Town: Chinle

Physical Address: Spider Rock Campground, Navajo Hwy 7, Chinle, AZ 86503

GPS Coordinates: 36.1083° N, 109.3507° W

Did You Know? Members of the Navajo Nation continue to live in Canyon de Chelly.

Cibecue Falls

This is one of the most secluded waterfalls in Arizona. The Cibecue Falls are located on the Tonto National Forest's eastern edge and within the Fort Apache Reservation. The trail to reach the falls is 3.5 to 4 miles, and some course sections can be problematic. The trail can be on the more difficult side, with a 400-foot elevation gain, significant steps on boulders, and stream crossings that can be hard to navigate. The Cibecue Falls path follows the creek and contains small swimming pools and waterfalls from large rocks in the water. The waterfall drops across the sandstone, and high red sandstone canyon walls surround the pool on both sides. It is located in the Cibecue Canyon and is fed by Cibecue Creek. During dry periods, the waterfall can dry up, so it's best to visit after a rainy season when the waterfall is the fullest. The 80-foot falls are full of mineral blue water that allows visitors to cool off after the hike. Besides viewing the falls, some trails follow along Cibecue Creek. When visiting Cibecue Falls, be aware of the weather and the dangers of flash flooding.

Best Time to Visit: April to October

Pass/Permit/Fees: $30 permit

Closest City or Town: Cibecue

Physical Address: Primitive Rd, Whiteriver, AZ 85941

GPS Coordinates: 33.8550° N, 110.5475° W

Did You Know? There is another waterfall nearby: the Apache Falls.

Arizona Copper Art Museum

Arizona's nickname is "The Copper State" because miners flooded the region in search of copper beginning in 1876. The third-largest copper mine in the world is in Arizona, and 60-70 percent of the nation's output is dug in the state. The Copper Art Museum in Clarkdale is filled with thousands of copper-related objects, some dating back to 3500 B.C. The museum was unofficially started in 1958 by John and Patricia Meinke from Minnesota, who was inspired by copper molds they saw in an antique store.

The museum is in a former high school, styled in Spanish Colonial Revival, containing more than 9,000 square feet of copper-related collections, including over 525 pieces of WW1 brass artillery shell casings, known as "trench art." Soldiers created this art by carving designs in the casings. Visitors to the museum will learn about the history of copper and the myths and lore surrounding the metal.

Best Time to Visit: Year-Round

Pass/Permit/Fees: $9.75

Closest City or Town: Clarkdale

Physical Address: Arizona Copper Art Museum, 849 Main St, Clarkdale, AZ 86324

GPS Coordinates: 34.7711° N, 112.0590° W

Did You Know? The city of Clarkdale was developed by Senator W.A. Clark, "America's Copper King."

Arizona Snowbowl

Located in the San Francisco Peaks, the Arizona Snowbowl is known for its ideal skiing and snowboarding conditions. The San Francisco Peaks are viewed as sacred by 13 different Native American tribes, including the Navajo, Apache, and Hopi. With an average snowfall amount of 260 inches, this mountain was more than suitable as a location for a ski resort. In 1938, the U.S. Forest Service approved the construction of the road and ski lodge on the mountain's western slope. Al Grassmoen purchased the Arizona Snowbowl in 1946 and built the Agassiz Lodge by hand; the original structure is still visible.

The resort has 55 runs, the longest being two miles, and eight lift systems. A rope towing system was used until the Riblet Lift was installed in 1962. The highest chair lift takes visitors to 11,500 feet in elevation but not to the top of the mountain to avoid backcountry skiing. During the summer, visitors can ride a gondola to the top for scenic views of Flagstaff.

Best Time to Visit: February and March

Pass/Permit/Fees: $79 full day, $59 half-day

Closest City or Town: Flagstaff

Physical Address: Snowbowl Parking Lot, 9300 N Snowbowl Rd, Flagstaff, AZ 86001

GPS Coordinates: 35.3309° N, 111.7103° W

Did You Know? This is one of only two ski resorts in Arizona.

Coconino Lava River Cave

Coconino Lava River Cave was formed over 700,000 years ago after a volcanic vent erupted near Hart Prairie. The lava cooled on the outside while it continued to flow inside, creating the cave. Unusual features include rippling lava fields, lava spirals, and decorative lava ropes. The cooling of the lava caused the surface of the cave to be smooth, which can be dangerous under icy conditions. The cave is 0.75 miles long, making it the longest lava cave in Arizona.

Even during the summer, the temperature of the cave is around 40 degrees Fahrenheit, so make sure you wear long sleeves and pants when visiting. The cave's height ranges from only 2 feet to over 30 feet high. Among the lava cave's unique features are the "Y-intersections," where two large tubes combine into one tube. Free camping is allowed at least one mile away from the entrance. From the parking lot to the entrance, the trail is only 0.4 miles. Visitors are advised to bring two or three sources of light in case one fails because there's no light source in the cave.

Best Time to Visit: May to September

Pass/Permit/Fees: Free to visit

Closest City or Town: Flagstaff

Physical Address: Coconino Lava River Cave, 171B Forest Rd, Flagstaff, AZ 86001

GPS Coordinates: 35.3424° N, 111.8363° W

Did You Know? The inside of the cave stays around 42 degrees even during the summer season.

Humphreys Peak

The highest natural point and the second highest peak in Arizona, Humphreys Peak, towers at 12,637 feet. This mountain is part of the highest group of dormant volcanic peaks, the San Francisco Peaks. The San Francisco Volcanic Field is made up of 600 volcanoes that range in age from 6 million years to 1,000 years old. Humphreys Peak is the tallest in the region and is an eroded stratovolcano.

Dokoo'osliid is the Navaho name for Humphreys Peak. It is one of the four sacred peaks in the Navajo culture, all part of their creation story. One of the most popular hikes to the peak, the North Kaibab Trail, is 4.8 miles one way. The peak is covered in snow during the winter months and is a favorite for many skiers. Camping is only allowed below 11,400 feet of elevation and not near the skiing slopes. Winds at the top of the mountain can gust over 50 mph.

Best Time to Visit: June to October

Pass/Permit/Fees: $5 to hike

Closest City or Town: Flagstaff

Physical Address: Trail to the Peak starts in the Snowbowl Parking lot at 9300 N Snowbowl Rd, Flagstaff, AZ 86001

GPS Coordinates: 35.3467° N, 111.6785° W

Did You Know? Local legend claims that Humphreys Peak is part of the San Francisco Peaks because people believe they can see San Francisco from the top – but this is not true.

Lowell Observatory

Founded in May 1894, the Lowell Observatory is one of the oldest in the United States. Astronomer Percival Lowell founded it, and the sole trusteeship is handed down throughout the Lowell family. The mission of the observatory is to "connect people to the universe through education, exploration, and discovery." It is most famous for the discovery of the dwarf planet Pluto in 1930 by Clyde Tombaugh. It was also used in 1963 for mapping the moon during the NASA Apollo Program.

The Lowell Observatory's Anderson Mesa dark-sky site is home to four research telescopes, including the Perkins Telescope, the John S. Hall Telescope, and the Navy Precision Optical Interferometer. The Clark Refracting Telescope is used for public and education tours. The three main exhibits are the Rotunda Museum, Putnam Collection Center, and the Giovale Open Deck Observation. By 2024, the Lowell Observatory plans to create an "open planetarium" to offer views of the night sky.

Best Time to Visit: Year-Round

Pass/Permit/Fees: $12 for adults

Closest City or Town: Flagstaff

Physical Address: Lowell Observatory, 1400 W Mars Hill Rd, Flagstaff, AZ 86001

GPS Coordinates: 35.2029° N, 111.6646° W

Did You Know? The observatory was able to track activity from the 1985 Comet Halley.

Museum of Northern Arizona

The Museum of Northern Arizona, founded in 1928 by zoologist Dr. Harold S. Colton and artist Mary-Russell Ferrell Colton, is located at the base of the San Francisco Peaks, a sacred homeland to the Native Americans of the region. The museum was created, in part, to help preserve their history and culture. The MNA is a private, non-profit organization that is supported by membership and supplemental funding.

Among the most popular exhibitions are women artists in north Arizona, archeology, and Southwestern jewelry. The museum is located on over 200 acres and has more than 5 million Native American artifacts and historical exhibitions. The archives department contains more than 300 manuscripts and 250,000 photos, and the library features 50,000 books and 25,000 collections of Native American newspapers. Outside the museum is the Watchable Wildlife Experience, where visitors can see deer, elk, foxes, and bats.

Best Time to Visit: Year-Round

Pass/Permit/Fees: $15

Closest City or Town: Flagstaff

Physical Address: Museum of Northern Arizona, 3101 N Fort Valley Rd, Flagstaff, AZ 86001

GPS Coordinates: 35.2345° N, 111.6656° W

Did You Know? Over 65,000 visitors come to the museum each year.

Riordan Mansion State Historic Park

The Riordan Mansion was built in northern Flagstaff by
brothers Timothy and Michael Riordan. They were in the
lumber industry and played a key role in developing the
Flagstaff region. The brothers married sisters Caroline and
Elizabeth Metz and built the mansion in 1904. Its 13,000
square feet includes two nearly identical wings, one for
each brother. The wings were connected by a large standard
room for the two families to meet.

The house was advanced for the time, including hot and
cold running water, electric lights, and even central heat.
The architect, Charles Whittlesey, also designed the El
Tovar Hotel at the Grand Canyon. In November 1978, the
house and the surrounding five acres of land became a part
of the Arizona state park. The automobile garage is another
historical exhibit. The home showcases early Stickley
furniture of interest to antique enthusiasts.

Best Time to Visit: March to May

Pass/Permit/Fees: $2

Closest City or Town: Flagstaff

Physical Address: Riordan Mansion State Historic Park,
409 W Riordan Rd, Flagstaff, AZ 86001

GPS Coordinates: 35.1877° N, 111.6580° W

Did You Know? The Riordan Mansion is one of the finest
examples of the American Arts and Crafts style of
architecture.

Route 66

The iconic American highway Route 66 has multiple stops in Arizona. Established in November 1926, this highway is one of the most famous in the country. Connecting Chicago with Los Angeles, it covers 2,448 miles and has been mentioned frequently in novels, movies, TV shows, and songs. Route 66 closed in 1985, leaving many towns along the route struggling.

One of the most popular attractions along the Arizona section of Route 66 is the Wigwam Motel. Wigwam was a chain of motels during the 1930s and 1940s; the only one remaining is in Holbrook, Arizona. American author John Steinbeck wrote of the Arizona section, "If the Grand Canyon is the beating heart of Arizona, then Route 66 is the main artery." While half of the original highway is gone, there are still 250 drivable miles remaining. The most extended section is west of Ash Fork. Throughout the remaining area, artifacts and historical landmarks detail the significance of the route in Arizona history.

Best Time to Visit: All year

Pass/Permit/Fees: Free

Closest City or Town: Flagstaff

Physical Address: The Museum Club at 3404 E Rte 66, Flagstaff, AZ 86004 was once a roadhouse during Route 66's peak.

GPS Coordinates: 35.2141° N, 111.5996° W

Did You Know? 401 miles of Route 66 are in Arizona.

Sedona

This small town near Flagstaff is home to vast natural rock formations. Visitors travel to Sedona to see the red rock mountains and to hike along trails that offer unique and vast views of the region including Bell Rock, Cathedral Rock, Devil's Bridge. Highway 179 is the best way to reach Phoenix from Sedona, and towering red rocks line the drive for the entire seven miles, earning the description "a museum without walls." Popular areas to visit on the highway are Bell Rock, Coconino National Forest, and the Village of Oak Creek. Many visitors travel to Sedona to experience vortices. For thousands of years, people have used this area as a place for spiritual healing, such as Airport Mesa, Cathedral Rock, Bell Rock, and Boynton Canyon. Many people practice yoga and other forms of meditation within these areas to experience the force of the vortices. Sedona is also surrounded by 1.8 million acres of national forest land.

Best Time to Visit: March to May; October to November

Pass/Permit/Fees: None, but permits might be needed for certain hiking trails.

Closest City or Town: Flagstaff

Physical Address: Sedona Chamber of Commerce Visitor Center, 311 Forest Rd., Sedona, AZ 86336

GPS Coordinates: 34.8697° N, 111.7610° W

Did You Know? The McDonald's in Sedona is the only one in the world with green arches, rather than the standard yellow, to avoid distracting from the natural landscape.

Walnut Canyon National Monument

Walnut Canyon is known for its extraordinary rock formations and the ancient pueblos nestled in the rock. The canyon sits on the Colorado Plateau and cuts through the Permian Kaibab Limestone, which gives it its cross-bedding. The limestone cliffs were created over 60 million years ago. The canyon has a diverse ecosystem, with cacti in the Upper Sonoran Desert, while the cool areas feature Douglas firs. Around the rim, you'll find juniper forest and ponderosa pines. Wildlife includes coyotes, elk, mountain lions, and 121 bird species. The Sinagua lived in the canyon from 1100 to 1250 AD. Remnants of the group are still preserved in the canyon, including 25 cliffside rooms. Walnut Canyon was given national monument status in 1915 by President Wilson to protect the historic cliff dwellings. There are multiple trails, with the Island Trail being one of the most popular because it showcases those dwelling rooms. The rooms were created by building clay walls to hold limestone rocks.

Best Time to Visit: March to October

Pass/Permit/Fees: Seven-day passes are $15 per person

Closest City or Town: Flagstaff

Physical Address: Walnut Canyon Visitors Center, Unnamed Road, Flagstaff, AZ 86004

GPS Coordinates: 35.1717° N, 111.5093° W

Did You Know? There are still black marks on the walls and ceilings on the cliff dwelling rooms from the Sinagua fires.

Wupatki National Monument

The Wupatki National Monument offers insight into the life of those who lived in the region thousands of years ago. Nestled between the Painted Desert and the ponderosa highlands, ancient pueblos are scattered over 35,422 acres of protected land. The oldest inhabited pueblos have been dated to 500 AD. A major population increase took place between 1040 and 1100, but the site had been abandoned by 1225. The Sinagua Pueblo is located within Wupatki. This pueblo, which has 100 rooms and a community room, is the most prominent building for over 50 miles. Several main ruins and at least 800 smaller ruins showcase the previous structures and pueblos.

The Wupatki Pueblo has many plants that are different from others in the region because it's 2,000 feet below sea level. The site was registered as a national historic place in 1966. Besides the ancient pueblo, there are volcanic and lava ruins from when the region was filled with volcanoes.

Best Time to Visit: March to October

Pass/Permit/Fees: $25 for vehicles, $20 for motorcycles

Closest City or Town: Flagstaff

Physical Address: Wupatki National Monument, 25137 N Wupatki Ln, Flagstaff, AZ 86004

GPS Coordinates: 35.5600° N, 111.3935° W

Did You Know? "Wupatki" means "tall house" in the Hopi language.

Hubbell Trading Post

The Hubbell Trading Post is the oldest operating trading post on the Navajo Nation; it has been selling goods and Native American artwork since 1878. This trading post was a meeting ground for the Navajo Tribe and early settlers. Also located on the grounds is the Hubbell Home, a one-story adobe-block house that was built in Southwestern New Mexico style. Construction began in 1898, with six bedrooms, and was finished in 1910 with a total of 11,500 square feet. John Lorenzo Hubbell bought the land in 1878, ten years after the Navajo people had been expelled from their land in New Mexico and Arizona. When they returned to this land, their fields had been destroyed, and an economic depression had begun, so the trading post became vital to their survival. The Navajos traded wool, jewelry, and baskets for traders' goods. In the 1960s, the Hubbell family sold the trading post to the National Park System. It is now operated by a non-profit organization that maintains the traditions of the Hubbell family.

Best Time to Visit: March to May

Pass/Permit/Fees: Free, $5 to enter the Hubbell Home

Closest City or Town: Ganado

Physical Address: Hubbell Trading Post, 523 W 2nd St, Winslow, AZ 86047

GPS Coordinates: 35.7095° N, 109.5587° W

Did You Know? Hubbell Trading Post was declared a National Historic Landmark in 1960.

Freestone District Park

Freestone District Park was the first significant district park in the Town of Gilbert. It features The Freestone Railroad, including a miniature trail, antique carousel, and a mini-Ferris wheel. These attractions were developed in 1992. Children can ride the miniature railroad that circles the northern lake and includes a 75-foot trestle that crosses over water. The park now has four lighted adult softball fields, two multi-use fields, four lighted full basketball courts, four lighted tennis courts, a skate park, an amphitheater, three reservable ramadas, and many more amenities.

Two lake areas in the park use reclaimed water to help support sustainability. The Community Fishing Program stocks the two lakes in September and October. A 2015 renovation created a wheelchair accessibility playground. This park is a favorite among families in the Phoenix area and visitors to the region.

Best Time to Visit: May to August

Pass/Permit/Fees: Free

Closest City or Town: Gilbert

Physical Address: Freestone District Park, 1045 E Juniper Ave, Gilbert, AZ 85234

GPS Coordinates: 33.3593° N and 111.7692° W

Did You Know? Water timers cool the sand on the volleyball courts.

Hale Centre Theatre

Nathan and Ruth Hale were young actors who married in 1933 and wrote, directed, produced and starred in community theater in the Salt Lake, Utah, area. In 1945, Nathan decided he wanted to become a movie star but found little success in Hollywood. The couple rented a small building in Glendale, California, and opened the Glendale Centre Theater. That became a family enterprise, and four Hale Centre Theaters are now operating in the U.S., run by Ruth and Nathan's children and grandchildren.

The Hale Centre Theater of Arizona was founded by David Dietlein, one of the grandsons, in Gilbert, Arizona. It opened in 2002 with seating for 380 people. A new theater opened in 2007 with a capacity of 522. The original theater still operates in Glendale, California, and two others are located in Utah. One of the community favorites is the yearly production of "A Christmas Carol" during the holiday season. The theater is located in central Gilbert and is close to many restaurants and bars.

Best Time to Visit: Year-Round

Pass/Permit/Fees: Price varies per show

Closest City or Town: Gilbert

Physical Address: Hale Centre Theatre, 50 W Page Ave, Gilbert, AZ 85233

GPS Coordinates: 33.3552° N, 111.7906° W

Did You Know? The first performance in Glendale played to an audience of only six people.

32

Riparian Preserve at Water Ranch

In 1986, the townspeople of Gilbert wanted to create a way to reuse 100% of its effluent water. The effort to develop water resources and to preserve the wildlife habitat led to the construction of the Riparian Preserve in 1999. The preserve covers 110 acres, with 70 acres taken up by seven water recharge basins that are filled on a rotating basis with treated effluent, which is then allowed to percolate into the aquifer, where it is stored for future use. The final purification of the water is done through marsh plants, microorganisms, and solar energy. The preserve has 298 species of birds and many species of insects, fish, amphibians, and mammals. More than 4.5 miles of trails are networked throughout the park, showcasing the wildlife and lakes. One of the most popular is the floating boardwalk, which allows an up-close view of fish and ducks. The most recent addition to the preserve is the Gilbert Rotary Centennial Observatory, which is available for a variety of public programs, offering a unique educational opportunity for visitors.

Best Time to Visit: March to May

Pass/Permit/Fees: Free

Closest City or Town: Gilbert

Physical Address: Riparian Preserve at Water Ranch, 2757 E Guadalupe Rd, Gilbert, AZ 85234

GPS Coordinates: 33.3644° N, 111.7347° W

Did You Know? There is a colorful light display every December for the holiday season.

Apache Falls

Located in the Salt River Canyon, the Apache Falls is popular due to its easy one-mile round-trip hike. The entire Salt River Canyon region contains 32,101 acres of land. Apache Falls is one of the highlights in the area, and it offers tubing, paddle boarding, and fishing. Apache Falls is part of a river that gives it ample water flow throughout the year, unlike other Arizona waterfalls that are part of a creek. The Salt River area is home to deer, fox, skunks, and even river otters.

After the winter snow and rain, the water flow is at its most powerful during the spring. The falls are located on the San Carlos Apache Tribe Reservation and can be reached from the White Mountain Apache Salt River Canyon Recreation Area. The falls are not very tall or impressive in comparison to others in the region, but the large swimming area around the falls is very popular, including for cliff jumping off the sides. The rock formations in the region offer significant steps and lounging space for visitors.

Best Time to Visit: May to October

Pass/Permit/Fees: $15 per vehicle

Closest City or Town: Globe

Physical Address: Apache Falls, US-60, San Carlos, AZ 85550

GPS Coordinates: 33.7982° N, 110.4968° W

Did You Know? This is one of the few river waterfalls in Arizona – most falls come from a creek.

34

Petrified Forest National Park

The Petrified Forest is located on 346 square miles of land known for its number of petrified trees, many of which are 225 million years old. The area was once full of trees and other plants until volcanic lava covered the region, preserving many trees later revealed by years of erosion. Many of the trees are petrified by quartz rock, which can be seen on the Crystal Forest Trail.

Many artifacts have been found in the region, including Puerco Pueblo, a village that is nearly 800 years old. Plants, reptiles, and even dinosaur fossils have been found and studied here. Some of the most popular areas to visit in the Petrified Forest are Giants Log Trail, Jasper Forest, and Crystal Forest Trail. There are multiple designated trails for visitors. The southern area of the park is known for the petrified trees, while the northern part hosts the Painted Desert.

Best Time to Visit: March to May and in October

Pass/Permit/Fees: $15 per bike, $20 per motorcycle, and $25 per vehicle

Closest City or Town: Holbrook

Physical Address: Painted Desert Visitor Center, 1 Park Rd., Petrified Forest National Park, AZ 86028

GPS Coordinates: 35.0037° N, 109.7889° W

Did You Know? President Theodore Roosevelt made the forest a National Monument in 1906.

White Pocket

Visitors to White Pocket will enjoy vast, swirling, colorful rock formations, including domes and ridges that stand out in this one-square-mile region. This remote location is in Vermilion Cliffs National Mountain, east of the Coyote Bluffs South. The area is only accessible by ATV or 4-wheel-drive vehicles because of the rugged terrain and deep sand dunes. The red and orange lateral lines rise over the bluffs and the near-white "cauliflower" rock formations.

Many agree that an earthquake triggered a sand slide, resulting in debris landing in the water, which turned it into the near bleached white shade. White Pocket features many unique rock formations, including one that looks similar to an egg. There are many native animals in the region, such as California condors. While hiking to White Pocket is not encouraged, driving an off-road vehicle is the safest option. Upon arrival at White Pocket, visitors can explore the extraordinary sites.

Best Time to Visit: March to May; September to October

Pass/Permit/Fees: No permit is required.

Closest City or Town: Jacob Lake

Physical Address: White Pocket Trailhead, BLM 1086, White Pocket, AZ, 86036

GPS Coordinates: 36.9561° N, 111.9043° W

Did You Know? In April and May, wildflowers are blooming, including different varieties of cactus.

Jerome

Known as the "Wickedest Town in the West," Jerome was founded in 1876. Because of the rich copper deposits, miners flooded the town until the Great Depression hit in 1929, and they left the area. The city was built on Cleopatra Hill, but by 1953, the mines were closed because the ore deposits were exhausted. Jerome became a National Historic Landmark in 1967 to protect the remaining buildings.

The Jerome Grand Hotel is often considered the most haunted place in Arizona because an estimated 9,000 people died while it served as a hospital. Jerome State Historic Park is a great way to explore the region's history. Douglas Mansion houses artifacts and photos, and the Mine Museum offers an insight into the history of mining that occurred in the area.

Best Time to Visit: December to May

Pass/Permit/Fees: Free

Closest City or Town: Jerome

Physical Address: Jerome Town Hall, 600 Clark St., Jerome, AZ 86331

GPS Coordinates: 34.7489° N, 112.1138° W

Did You Know? The Mine Museum has over 11,000 photos and archives in its collection.

Monument Valley

Monument Valley, *Tsé Bii' Ndzisgaii* in Navajo, which translates to "valley of rocks," is made up of sandstone buttes, mesas, and cliff rock formations. These mammoth buttes rise to over 1,000 feet above the desert floor. The valley offers multiple hiking trails and the option to drive your car on a self-guided tour. Over 50 million years of natural erosion by wind and water resulted in the height of the buttes. Geologists have been able to study the region's four rock formations: Organ Rock Shale, De Chelly Sandstone, Moenkopi, and Shinarump. The bright red color of iron oxide leaves the valley with a unique color scheme. The valley and buttes have been inhabited since the Anasazi people in 1300. The Navajo people later inhabited this region and remain there today. Monument Valley in the Navajo Nation Reservation encompasses nearly 92,000 acres of land. The region is not a national park but rather a Navajo Tribal Park.

Best Time to Visit: April to May; September to October

Pass/Permit/Fees: $10 per person or $20 per vehicle

Closest City or Town: Kayenta

Physical Address: Monument Valley Tribal Park Visitor Center, U.S. 163 Scenic, Oljato-Monument Valley, AZ 84536

GPS Coordinates: 36.9980° N, -110.0985° W

Did You Know? *Forrest Gump* was filmed along Route 163 — the iconic running scene showcased Monument Valley in the background.

London Bridge

Initially built in the 1830s, this bridge was located in London for nearly 150 years, connecting the two banks of the River Thames. By 1962, the bridge was not strong enough to support the increased car traffic and was sold by the City of London to help fund the new bridge. It was disassembled and shipped to Lake Havasu City. Sending and assembling the bridge and dredging the channel cost $7 million. Robert P. McCulloch Sr. was developing a planned community and thought this historic bridge would add value to the new land.

The reconstruction was officially completed in 1971, and the bridge then linked an island in the Colorado River with the main section of Lake Havasu City. The rebuilt bridge has a steel framework that reduced its weight from 130,000 tons to 30,000 and also strengthened the structure to accommodate the expected automobile traffic. London Bridge is now the second most visited tourist location in Arizona behind the Grand Canyon.

Best Time to Visit: March to May

Pass/Permit/Fees: None

Closest City or Town: Lake Havasu City

Physical Address: London Bridge Arizona, 1340 McCulloch Blvd, Lake Havasu City, AZ 86403

GPS Coordinates: 34.4716° N, 114.3475° W

Did You Know? The bridge was purchased for $2.46 million.

Cosanti Foundation

The owner of the Cosanti Foundation is famed sculpture artist Paolo Soleri (1919-2013), who took an anti-materialist stance in his work, including the building that housed his studio, and it is now a designated Arizona Historic Site. Soleri created a theory of "arcology," a combination of "architecture" and "ecology." The Cosanti Foundation was created in 1965 to promote minimal negative effects on the environment.

One of Soleri's most famous pieces is the Cosanti Windbells; the original casts of the bronze and ceramic bells can be seen in the house. The Cosanti house is located on 5 acres of land in a residential neighborhood. The land was initially purchased for $12,000 as a wedding gift to Soleri and his wife. The Cosanti Foundation house offers its sculptures and oddly spaced rooms to help visitors understand Soleri's creative process and insights into his workspace.

Best Time to Visit: Year-Round

Pass/Permit/Fees: Free

Closest City or Town: Mayer

Physical Address: Cosanti Foundation, HC 74 Box 4136, Mayer, AZ 86333

GPS Coordinates: 34.3420° N, 112.1019° W

Did You Know? You can also take tours of Arcosanti, one of Soleri's large-scale projects, near Mayer in Central Arizona.

Joshua Forest Scenic Road

Starting in the small town of Wickenburg, Arizona, the Joshua Forest Scenic Road leads you on a three-hour tour on your way to the Joshua Tree Forest in Meadview. Joshua Trees, known as *hunuvat chiy'a* to the Native Cahuilla people, have been used for centuries to weave baskets and clothing and create red dye from their roots. The seeds of the tree are actually large berries that can be cracked open and eaten.

Mile markers on Highway 93 designate scenic byways, and there are short hiking trails at mile markers 22.4 and 27. Both areas have spots for picnics. Along the road, drivers can also stop to hike to Ives Peak and Black Canyon Wash (mile marker 36.6) or visit the Nothing, AZ, ghost town (mile marker 50.8). The seven-mile stretch between Wickenburg and Wikieup contains the most Joshua Trees.

Best Time to Visit: March to May; October to November

Pass/Permit/Fees: Free

Closest City or Town: Meadview

Physical Address: Drive starts at the traffic circle in Wickenburg on Hwy 93, Wickenburg, AZ 85390

GPS Coordinates: 35.8619° N, 114.0839° W

Did You Know? Captain John C. Fremont is known for penning the first written record of Joshua Trees, describing them as "the most repulsive tree in the vegetable kingdom."

Tumacácori National Historical Park

This 360-acre historical park is made up of three significant ruins, two of which are marked as National Historic Landmark sites. When Spanish explorers arrived, they built the first Spanish Colonial Jesuit mission on this land in 1691, when Jesuit Eusebio Francisco Kino arrived on the O'odham people's territory, leading to issues between the two groups for hundreds of years. The Mission San Cayetano de Tumacácori and Mission Los Santos Ángeles de Guevavi are two of the oldest missions in southern Arizona. Two more missions on the park were built in the 1750s. President Theodore Roosevelt had this land protected as the Tumacácori National Monument in 1908, and the Tumacácori National Museum was built in 1937 by Scofield Delong. The museum, designed in Mission Revival style architecture with Spanish Colonial details, was declared a National Historic Landmark in 1987.

Best Time to Visit: The La Fiesta de Tumacácori Festival is held annually in December.

Pass/Permit/Fees: $10 Adult, children free

Closest City or Town: Nogales, Arizona

Physical Address: Tumacácori National Historical Park, 1891 I-19 Frontage Rd, Tumacacori-Carmen, AZ 85640

GPS Coordinates: 31.5681° N, 111.0506° W

Did You Know? This park is designated an International Dark Sky Park – the low level of light pollution allows astronomers and stargazers to see stars not visible in other areas.

Antelope Canyon

Antelope Canyon is known for its iconic images of light beams shining through and its unparalleled sandstone formations. The canyon was formed by erosion due to flash flooding and heavy rainy seasons that wore away the sandstone, creating deep corridors with smoothed edges. The inside of the canyon has many organic, flowing-like shapes on walls that are 120 feet high.

Antelope Canyon is divided into the upper and lower canyons, under protection by the LeChee Chapter of the Navajo Nation. Only guided tours via the Navajo Nation are allowed. The Navajo know the Upper Antelope Canyon as "the place where water runs through rocks" and the lower canyon as "spiral rock arches." The name "antelope" comes from a Navajo story about antelopes that grazed in the canyon during the winter months. The pronghorn antelopes can still be found grazing in the region.

Best Time to Visit: March to October

Pass/Permit/Fees: $80

Closest City or Town: Page

Physical Address: Antelope Canyon Navajo Tours Address, Hwy 98, Milepost 299, Page, AZ 86040

GPS Coordinates: 36.8619° N, 111.3743° W

Did You Know? In 2014, the photograph *Phantom* by Peter Lik, taken in Upper Antelope Canyon, sold for a world-record amount of $6.5 million.

Glen Canyon National Recreation Area

Glen Canyon National Recreation Area covers over 1.25 million acres of land in Utah and Arizona. The area includes famed Lake Powell, the second-largest manmade lake in the United States created in 1963 along with the Glen Canyon Dam. As with the Grand Canyon, the Colorado River carved out the region's unique rock formations. The area is known for its exciting outdoor activities, from swimming and boating to off-roading around the mountain region. One of the best ways to experience the natural wonders is by boat, canoe, or kayak. Deep caves and caverns, created by years of water and wind erosion, can be seen from the water in addition to almost 40 layers of sedimentary rocks with deep red hues. The park's size allows visitors and campers to spend multiple days exploring the natural landmarks. Hikers travel to Glen Canyon to discover wonders such as Rainbow Bridge, Horseshoe Bend, and Reflection Canyon.

Best Time to Visit: March to May; September to November

Pass/Permit/Fees: Week-long permits are $14 for vehicles and $7 for bikes or motorcycles

Closest City or Town: Page

Physical Address: Glen Canyon Dam, US-89, Page, AZ 86040

GPS Coordinates: 36.9372° N, 111.4837° W

Did You Know? The dam built inside Glen Canyon is 583 feet high and 1,560 feet wide.

Horseshoe Bend

One of the most photographed locations on the Colorado River, the Horseshoe Bend overlook is 1,000 feet above the river below, which turns around the edge like a horseshoe with a 270-degree bend. The bend is only five miles downstream from Glen Canyon Dam and Lake Powell and was formed due to the Navajo sandstone, which acted as a natural barrier, forcing the river to make a sharp turn. The rock formations around the bend are made up of multiple minerals, including hematite, platinum, and garnet. The hike to the overlook is less than one mile, with the option of taking a boat tour around the bend for a different perspective. The Colorado River's blue-green color is due to the extremely low water temperature — averaging 40°F. Horseshoe Bend is under the Glen Canyon National Recreation Area's watch and is managed by the National Park Service. These organizations have been working to make this spot safe and a great experience.

Best Time to Visit: March to October

Pass/Permit/Fees: $10 per car, $5 per motorcycle

Closest City or Town: Page

Physical Address: Horseshoe Bend Overlook Parking Lot, Page, AZ 86040

GPS Coordinates: 36.8791° N, 111.5104° W

Did You Know? The Colorado River is bound to eventually cut through the sandstone and create a natural bridge over time, but this will ruin the iconic horseshoe shape.

Labyrinth Slot Canyon

Located on the Green River, this slot canyon is reachable only by kayak or paddleboard. It is one of the most popular slot canyons in the Antelope Canyon. Walls reach up to 30 feet tall, and the canyon is almost one mile deep. The smooth sandstone walls are prime examples of the natural erosion by rivers. The entrance to the canyon is nearly 11 miles from the closest marina on Lake Powell. The canyon was accessible by foot before the creation of Lake Powell in 1972. While the mouth of the canyon is in Utah, the rest of it is in Arizona. Labyrinth Slot Canyon is an excellent alternative to Antelope Canyon, where lines can be very long, and you have to pay to visit. You can kayak or paddleboard through some sections until the walls get too thin or the water runs dry. Slot canyons are very rare. They are formed after millions of years of water rushing past either sand or limestone. For those nervous about navigating to and from the canyon alone, many tours are available.

Best Time to Visit: May to September

Pass/Permit/Fees: Only marine fees to park

Closest City or Town: Page

Physical Address: Buoy No. 18, Lake Powell, AZ 86040. Labyrinth Slot Canyon is narrow and can only be accessed by kayak or canoe.

GPS Coordinates: 34.5849.18° N, 101.557.6° W

Did You Know? Many of the slot canyons in North America are located in Arizona.

46

Lake Powell

Lake Powell was created in 1963 after the Glen Canyon Dam's construction left the area covered in hundreds of feet of water. It is the second-largest human-made lake in the United States, taking 17 years to reach its current depth and capacity of 27,000,000 cubic feet of water. The area surrounding Lake Powell was formed by sandstone erosion over 5 million years ago. The lake was named after John Wesley Powell, a veteran of the American Civil War, who explored the region in 1869.

Lake Powell is known for water activities, camping on the shore, many unique rock shapes, and fishing for many species of fish. The land around the lake offers various hiking trails for further exploration of the sandstone rocks, including the nearby Rainbow Bridge, one of the largest natural bridges in the world. Due to the steep cliff sides surrounding the lake, entrances are limited to just five areas: two in Arizona and three in Utah.

Best Time to Visit: May to August

Pass/Permit/Fees: Seven-day passes are $30.

Closest City or Town: Page

Physical Address: Carl Hayden Visitor Center, US-89, Page, AZ 86040

GPS Coordinates: 37.0683° N, 111.2433° W

Did You Know? The lake has nearly 2,000 miles of shoreline, which is almost the same as the entire west coast of the United States.

The Wave

Some of the most famous sandstone rock formations in the Southwest are at The Wave. Located in the Coyotes Buttes North area, this region has many unparalleled rock sites, including The Second Wave, Top Rock Arch, and Sand Cove. A three-mile hike one way is required to reach The Wave. Visitors must use a map or GPS to reach The Wave, which can be challenging for beginner navigators.

The Wave is known for its rock formations that appear similar to ocean waves. Two major troughs formed 190 million years ago. The lines within the troughs were formed by water flowing at different rates, and the tiny ridges were formed by alternating wind erosion. The winds during the Jurassic Period created deeply colored hues as manganese and iron were deposited.

Best Time to Visit: Most likely to get a hiking permit between December and February

Pass/Permit/Fees: Daily permit required, $9 per group

Closest City or Town: Page

Physical Address: Contact the Arizona Bureau of Land Management (BLM) for tour lotteries. Current contact information is available online.

GPS Coordinates: 37.0424° N, 112.5122° W

Did You Know? Only 20 people per day are allowed to hike to The Wave.

Vermilion Cliffs National Monument

This unspoiled and protected wilderness area contains 280,000 acres of land, including the Paria Plateau, Vermilion Cliffs, and Coyote Buttes. The elevation in the region ranges from 3,100 to 6,500 feet above sea level. The Vermilion Cliffs are an escarpment formation made of sandstone, siltstone, limestone, and shale that tower above the valley floor. The entire region is full of bright-colored sandstone due to iron-rich oxide pigments.

Coyote Buttes Trail is one of the most popular and demanding hiking trails, with 24 miles that can take over 11 hours to complete. The region is also home to the Paria Canyon, a slot canyon. There are two state-created campgrounds, but free camping on the Bureau of Land Management is also a popular choice.

Best Time to Visit: March to May; September to October

Pass/Permit/Fees: $10 per vehicle; some trails require a permit

Closest City or Town: Page

Physical Address: Camping and hiking in Vermilion Cliffs require a permit obtained at the Paria Contact Station, 2040 Long Valley Rd, Kanab, UT 84741.

GPS Coordinates: 36.8625° N, 111.8270° W

Did You Know? The region is home to the endangered California condors, but through a hatch and raising/breeding program, the condor population is growing.

Havasupai Indian Reservation

The Havasupai Reservation is home to the Supai Village and three famous waterfalls: Havasu, Mooney, and Beaver Falls. A fourth waterfall existed until a flood in 2008 destroyed the Navajo Falls. The tribe has lived in the region for over 800 years. Located southwest of the Grand Canyon National Park, Havasupai is a popular location for hiking. To protect the area, the Havasupai Reservation started a lottery program to limit those allowed to hike to the falls.

The Havasu Falls is famed for the drastic colors of the red rock as the bright blue water rushes down the rock face. Beaver Falls is lesser known because it is farther away but ideal for those looking to swim in natural pools. A small dam was created on Havasu Creek to protect the falls and pools from flooding.

Best Time to Visit: March to May; September to October

Pass/Permit/Fee: Permits are needed to hike to any of the falls. Three-day passes are between $300-$400 per person

Closest City or Town: Peach Springs

Physical Address: Hualapai Hilltop Parking Lot, Indian Route 18, Supai, AZ 86435. Visitors must hike the rest of the way (eight miles) to the visitors' center and campground.

GPS Coordinates: 36.2333° N, 112.7007° W

Did You Know? The Supai Village is the only place in the United States that gets its mail by mule.

Arizona Capitol Museum

When Arizona became a U.S. state in 1912, Phoenix became the new state capital, just as it had been the capital of the territory, and the territorial capitol building became the state capitol building. James Riely Gordon won a contest to design the building. Construction began in 1898 and was completed in 1901. Many of the building materials were sourced from native Arizona materials, including malapai stone and granite. Thick stone walls help insulate the building against the intense Arizona heat. Between 1918 and 1938, the building gained an additional 80,000 square feet. The three floors of the museum cover 123,000 square feet and include the governor's office, Supreme Court, and legislative chambers.

More than 20 exhibits showcase modern and historical artifacts that reflect Arizona's history. One exhibit highlights the *USS Arizona*, one of the ships attacked by the Japanese at Pearl Harbor in 1941.

Best Time to Visit: March to June

Pass/Permit/Fees: Free

Closest City or Town: Phoenix

Physical Address: Arizona Capitol Museum, 1700 W Washington St, Phoenix, AZ 85007

GPS Coordinates: 33.4481° N, 112.0992° W

Did You Know? The flag used by President Teddy Roosevelt's Rough Riders is on display at the museum.

Arizona Science Center

Located in the *Heritage and Science Park* in central Phoenix, the science center is home to over 350 permanent hands-on exhibitions that draw in 400,000 annual visitors. The Arizona Science Center offers shows daily in the Dorrance Planetarium and a five-story tall IMAX theater. The center was designed in 1980 and opened to the public in 1984 as a small storefront. During the first year, the museum attracted 87,000 visitors; some of the original exhibits are still on display.

The new facility offers more exhibitions and classrooms for education programs across 140,000 square feet. Since the new location opened in 1997, over three million patrons have visited the center. Some of the most popular permanent exhibitions are "Get Charged Up," "Solarville," and "Forces of Nature.' The IMAX theater offers high-quality scientific documentaries about space, oceans, and other science topics. The Arizona Science Center is a place of fun and education for children and adults.

Best Time to Visit: Year-Round

Pass/Permit/Fees: $20 for adults, $15 for children

Closest City or Town: Phoenix

Physical Address: Arizona Science Center, 600 E Washington St, Phoenix, AZ 85004

GPS Coordinates: 33.4485° N, 112.0683° W

Did You Know? Antoine Predock designed the building.

Camelback Mountain

Camelback is one of the most famous mountains in the Phoenix region, with exceptional views of the city. It is located in the city itself, surrounded by homes and businesses. The mountain towers 2,704 feet over the area; the hike to the top is 1.5 miles one way and has an elevation of 1,264 feet. There are two main trails – the Echo Canyon Trail and the Cholla Trail, each taking around 3 hours. The elevation will make it challenging for beginner hikers, but there are alternative hikes, including Bobby's Rock Trail that circles the base of the mountain. Camelback Mountain is a holy site for the Native Americans who live in the Salt River Valley. "Praying Monk" can be seen where the red sandstone formation looks like a man kneeling in prayer. The mountain was a reservation spanning over a million acres for the Salt River Pima and the Maricopa Native Americans. Geologists concluded that it is made up of two separate rock formations: Precambrian granite and sandstone.

Best Time to Visit: March to May; October to November

Pass/Permit/Fees: $10 for parking

Closest City or Town: Phoenix, Arizona

Physical Address: Echo Canyon Recreation Area and Trailhead leads to Camelback Mountain from 4925 E McDonald Dr, Phoenix, AZ 85018

GPS Coordinates: 33.5151° N, 111.9619° W

Did You Know? The record for the fastest ascent to the top was 16 minutes, set by a 19-year-old male.

Children's Museum of Phoenix

The Children's Museum of Phoenix is a unique place to explore and be creative. The museum was founded in 1998 as the Phoenix Family Museum. Three years later, voters approved a $10.5 million bond issue to buy the historic Monroe School and adapt it as a new home for the renamed Children's Museum of Phoenix.

The museum is designed for children under ten and has over 48,000 square feet of exploration space. Some of the most popular exhibits are the Art Studio, BlockMania, Build Big, and the Book Loft. The Art Studio is filled with hands-on art activities to build small motor skills and fine-tune hand-eye coordination. The BlockMania exhibition uses blocks of all sizes and textures to help develop balance and spatial awareness. The museum also offers classes and programs for children, including art, music, and STEM. The Children's Museum of Phoenix has been rated one of the top 10 in the country.

Best Time to Visit: Year-Round

Pass/Permit/Fees: $16

Closest City or Town: Phoenix

Physical Address: Children's Museum of Phoenix, 215 N 7th St, Phoenix, AZ 85034

GPS Coordinates: 33.4504° N, 112.0646° W

Did You Know? American Artist Jackson Pollock attended the Monroe School.

Desert Botanical Garden

The Desert Botanical Garden in Phoenix encompasses 55 acres of land. Created in 1937 by the Arizona Cactus and Native Flora Society, the garden now has 50,000 plants, including 379 rare, endangered, or threatened species. The garden holds a seed bank that stores frozen seeds and pollen to help regenerate rare species. Over two-thirds of the total species of cactus are in the garden's collection.

Plants from around the world thrive in the desert here. Besides native plants, there are also many pieces of natural sculptures that incorporate plant life. After sunset, lanterns, and lights illuminate the paths around the grounds. The park has a network of trails that are split into quarter-mile loops, leading into one main track. The tracks are themed with different topics, such as conservation, desert plants, desert wildflowers, and a section on the people of the Sonoran Desert.

Best Time to Visit: All year

Pass/Permit/Fees: $25 per adult

Closest City or Town: Phoenix

Physical Address: Desert Botanical Garden, 1201 N Galvin Pkwy, Phoenix, AZ 85008

GPS Coordinates: 33.4618° N, 111.9446° W

Did You Know? The creeping devil cactus was the first cactus planted in 1939.

Hall of Flame Museum of Firefighting

When George Getz Jr. received a 1924 American La France Type 12 pumper fire truck as a Christmas present, it began a private collection of firefighting memorabilia and artifacts that became the original Hall of Flame Museum that opened in Lake Geneva, Wisconsin, in 1961. When the Getz family moved to Scottsdale in 1971, Getz decided to move the museum, too. The museum houses five exhibition galleries, a theater, and a Hall of Heroes room that opened in 1998 to honor firefighters who died in the line of duty or have been decorated for acts of heroism.

Gallery I is dedicated to hand and horse-drawn apparatus from 1725 to 1908, and Gallery II has motorized apparatus from 1897 to 1930, along with a children's play area. Gallery III contains rotating exhibits of restored motorized pieces. The highlight of Gallery IV is a fully restored 1930 Ahrens-Fox Quad fire engine that is driven annually in the Fiesta Bowl Parade.

Best Time to Visit: Year-round

Pass/Permit/Fees: $7 for adults, $5 for children

Closest City or Town: Phoenix

Physical Address: Hall of Flame Museum of Firefighting, 6101 E Van Buren St, Phoenix, AZ 85008

GPS Coordinates: 33.4474° N, 111.9534° W

Did You Know? There are 10,000 pieces of fire equipment dating from 1725 to 1969.

Heard Museum

Maie Bartlett Heard founded the Heard Museum in 1929, a few months after her husband Dwight Heard passed away. Their collection of American Indian art has long since won international attention. During its early years, the museum was a gathering place for local enthusiasts and an educational site for children. In 1956 the Heard Museum Auxiliary was established to help with educational programs. A major expansion in 1967 added the museum's first collections storage area, an auditorium, and two floors of galleries. A second significant expansion in 1983 nearly doubled the museum's size to 78,000 square feet.

The Heard Museum's collection offers many works that detail the history and culture of Native American art and artists. The museum's outdoor gallery and performing space includes water features, sculptures, and an amphitheater. The Heard belongs to the Smithsonian affiliate program, which helps with education programs.

Best Time to Visit: Year-Round

Pass/Permit/Fees: $20 for adults, $9 for children

Closest City or Town: Phoenix

Physical Address: Heard Museum, 301 N Central Ave, Phoenix, AZ 85004

GPS Coordinates: 33.4725° N, 112.0722° W

Did You Know? There are over 40,000 items in the collection.

Musical Instrument Museum

The Musical Instrument Museum, which opened in 2010, is the largest museum of its kind in the world, with over 200 countries and territories represented by 15,000 musical instruments used for ethnic, folk, and tribal music. The museum contains 200,000 square feet, with two floors of gallery space. It was founded by Robert J. Ulrich, the former CEO of Target Corporation, who was inspired by a visit to a musical instrument museum in Belgium.

Each exhibit features a video showcasing the history of the instruments and musicians performing them. A 299-seat theater hosts concerts and the art gallery features photographs, performance outfits, and instruments of famed artists. The STEM Gallery allows guests to explore connections between music and science, technology, engineering, and mathematics. Among the gallery's pieces are a sanxian from China, a dragon khuur from Mongolia, and a nickelodeon piano player from the United States.

Best Time to Visit: Year-Round

Pass/Permit/Fees: $20 for adults, $15 for teens, $10 for children

Closest City or Town: Phoenix

Physical Address: Musical Instrument Museum, 4725 E Mayo Blvd, Phoenix, AZ 85050

GPS Coordinates: 52.5103° N, 13.3711° E

Did You Know? The museum hosts 200 concerts each year.

Oasis Water Park

Tucked away at the Arizona Grand Resort is the Oasis Water Park. Eight-story high-speed water slides twist across seven acres of desert, and there is a hot tub big enough for 25 people. The rest of the pools are heated to stay at 80°F year-round. Wild Cat Springs is made for little ones who aren't tall enough for the slides and adults who want to relax. There's also a wave pool, lazy river, and cabanas available for rent. The park is available to host parties and special events.

If you make a stay of it, the inclusive resort features a spa, restaurants, and a golf course. Nearby, hikers can take advantage of the Pima Canyon and South Mountain trailheads that can be reached by car in under 10 minutes.

Best Time to Visit: May to September

Pass/Permit/Fees: Day passes start at $40 per adult, $30 per child

Closest City or Town: Phoenix

Physical Address: Oasis Water Park, 8000 Arizona Grand Pkwy, Phoenix, AZ 85044

GPS Coordinates: 36.2322° N, 115.6461° W

Did You Know? Oasis is rated as one of the top ten water parks in the country by the Travel Channel.

Papago Park

Covering over 1200 acres in Phoenix and 296 acres in Tempe, this park features many geological formations along with desert plants, a giant saguaro cactus, the Desert Botanical Garden, and the Phoenix Zoo. It is full of hiking trails, bike paths, and several small lakes. The ponds have an average depth of 8 feet and contain many fish species, including rainbow trout, largemouth bass, and channel catfish.

Hole-in-the-Rock Trail features a main chamber looking out over nearby lagoons and the distant downtown skyline. The formation is thought to have been used by the ancient Hohokam civilization to track the position of the sun through a hole in the rock ceiling. The trail offers magnificent views of downtown Phoenix and Tempe and incredible sandstone formations. A bass fish hatchery was created in Papago Park in 1932 as a Works Progress Administration project, helping stock largemouth bass and other fish populations in the Arizona waterways.

Best Time to Visit: March to June

Pass/Permit/Fees: Free

Closest City or Town: Phoenix

Physical Address: West Buttes Parking Lot, Papago Park Rd, Phoenix, AZ 85008

GPS Coordinates: 33.4540° N, 111.9506° W

Did You Know? The Finish Line for the fourth season of *The Amazing Race* was shot at Papago Park.

Phoenix Art Museum

Located in the city center, the Phoenix Art Museum is one of the most significant visual arts museums in the Southwest, with more than 285,000 square feet of exhibits and art. The museum boasts collections showcasing artists from America, Europe, Latin America, and Asia, as well as a vast array of art styles, including fashion design. It opened in 1959, but the collection had begun in 1915 when the Phoenix Women's Club purchased Carl Oscar Borg's painting *Egyptian Evening* for $125 and donated it to the city of Phoenix to start a community art collection. Some of the most prized pieces are by Claude Monet, Pablo Picasso, and Ernest Lawson.

Under the Works Progress Administration's Federal Art Project, the Phoenix Art Center was created in 1936, which led to the museum's foundation. The heirs of Adolphus Clay Bartlett donated the land for the future museum in 1940.

Best Time to Visit: Year-Round

Pass/Permit/Fees: $20 for adults

Closest City or Town: Phoenix

Physical Address: Phoenix Art Museum, 1625 N Central Ave, Phoenix, AZ 85004

GPS Coordinates: 33.4674° N, 112.0734° W

Did You Know? There are more than 19,000 pieces of art in the museum's collection.

Phoenix Zoo

Robert E. Maytag of the Maytag appliance family called some friends together in 1961 to organize the Arizona Zoological Society. Despite Maytag's untimely death in March of the following year, the society persisted in its goal of establishing a zoo. The Maytag Zoo opened on 125 acres of land in Phoenix's Papago Park in November 1962 and was renamed the Phoenix Zoo in 1963 to encourage community support. With over 3000 animals representing more than 400 species, the zoo is divided into four themed trails. Among the most popular animals are the Sonoran pronghorn, Masai giraffes, and Komodo dragons. Also on the zoo's property is the Hunt Bass Hatchery House which was built as a Works Progress Administration project in 1936. The zoo has mounted several significant conservation efforts, including captive breeding to reintroduce the Arabian oryx, black-foot ferret, and Mexican wolf, which increased their numbers in the wild. A sanctuary at the zoo has helped rehabilitate animals for their release.

Best Time to Visit: February to June

Pass/Permit/Fees: $25 for adults, $15 for children

Closest City or Town: Phoenix

Physical Address: Phoenix Zoo, 455 N Galvin Pkwy, Phoenix, AZ 85008

GPS Coordinates: 33.4519° N, 111.9490° W

Did You Know? The zoo was able to help reintroduce the Arabian Oryx back into the wild.

Pioneer Living History Museum

This open-air museum is located among the black rock foothills of Northern Phoenix. Thirty historical buildings that were built from the late 1880s and early 1900s form the Pioneer Village. In 1956, local history enthusiasts were worried that the buildings would be destroyed. The group created the Pioneer Arizona Foundation, Inc., to protect them. Some members included Governor Paul Fannin, and Senators Barry Goldwater, Carl Hayden, and Wesley Bolin. The foundation purchased the museum and 90 acres of surrounding protected land. The museum officially opened in 1969, and the *Exhibition Hall Firearms, Tools, Locks & Keys* museum was founded. There are 15 structures that have been reconstructed, including the Sears Victorian House, which was one of the original buildings from the 1890s. Among the reconstructed buildings is the Blacksmith Shop, originally built in 1870. The museum hosts bluegrass festivals and Civil War reenactments. The famous singer Lilly Langtry once performed at the opera house on the grounds.

Best Time to Visit: March to May

Pass/Permit/Fees: Adults $10, Children $8

Closest City or Town: Phoenix

Physical Address: Pioneer Arizona Living History Museum, 3901 W Pioneer Rd, Phoenix, AZ 85086

GPS Coordinates: 33.8198° N, 112.1489° W

Did You Know? The childhood home of Henry F. Ashurst, one of Arizona's first two senators, is at the museum.

South Mountain Park

Located outside of Phoenix, South Mountain Park covers 16,000 acres and is one of the largest municipal parks in the country. It offers an Education Center, hiking, biking, and riding trails that stretch for over 58 miles. One of the most popular trails is the Dobbins Lookout, measuring 2,330 feet in elevation, which makes it the park's highest point. The South Mountains were formed when the North American tectonic plates collided with each other.

Another popular feature in the park is Mystery Castle, at the foothills of the northern side. It was built in the 1930s as a private residence. The park contains many saguaros, opuntia, and creosote bushes and celebrates "Silent Sunday" each week when the main road is closed, allowing visitors to walk it. South Mountain Park is popular among locals and ideal for exploring native Phoenix plants and land. Because there are many blind corners, narrow sections, and treacherous drop-offs, hikers, bikers, and drivers should maintain extreme caution.

Best Time to Visit: March to May

Pass/Permit/Fees: Free

Closest City or Town: Phoenix

Physical Address: South Mountain Park, 10919 S Central Ave, Phoenix, AZ 85042

GPS Coordinates: 33.3403° N, 112.0609° W

Did You Know? South Mountain is 2690 feet high.

Fossil Creek Falls

Fossil Creek Falls is popular among locals to help escape the summer heat. Located between Coconino and Tonto National Forest, Fossil Creek Falls is in the Fossil Creek Canyon. The canyon is 1,600 feet deep, and Fossil Creek Falls emits 20,000 gallons of water per minute, staying around 72°F year-round. The water in the creek is full of calcium carbonate and flows from a spring, creating travertine (limestone deposit) dams downstream.

The creek's water supply supports a wide variety of plants and animals. In 2008, barriers were created to help reduce the number of invasive species being introduced to help maximize the number of native fish that thrive in the creek. The trail to reach Fossil Creek is 2.6 miles round trip and easy for all hiking levels. The falls have deep pools, and many use the creek for swimming, kayaking, and snorkeling. Some people even jump off the 25-foot cliff.

Best Time to Visit: May to October

Pass/Permit/Fees: $6 per vehicle

Closest City or Town: Pine

Physical Address: Fossil Creek Waterfall Trail Parking Lot, Fossil Creek Road, Pine, AZ 85544

GPS Coordinates: 34.4052° N, 111.6108° W

Did You Know? Fossil Creek is one of the two streams in all of Arizona that is included in the National Wild and Scenic Rivers System.

Tonto Natural Bridge

This unique natural wonder is known for its one-of-a-kind bridges, including the largest travertine bridge in the world. Millions of years of volcanic lava, seawater, and erosion formed a travertine dam. Water seeping through the dam's limestone and calcium carbonate eventually created the natural bridge. The bridge is 183 feet high and has tunnels over 400 feet long; the widest point is 150 feet. Located in the Tonto National Forest, this park is great for hiking. At the opening of the bridge, a natural waterfall is created by spring rainfalls.

Three hiking trails lead to the bridge, and each trail showcases the park's different wonders. It takes two hours to reach most courses. For those not wanting to hike, the bridge is visible from the car parking lot. Hikers can explore underneath the natural bridge. Tonto Natural Forest State Park is one of the smallest in the state at 161 acres. The region near the bridge is lusher than other locations because its high elevation allows for more snow melting.

Best Time to Visit: March to May; September to October

Pass/Permit/Fees: $7 per adult

Closest City or Town: Pine

Physical Address: Nf-583A, Tonto Natural Bridge Rd, Pine, AZ 85544

GPS Coordinates: 34.3348° N, 111.4210° W

Did You Know? The bridge was discovered in 1877 by a Scottish prospector, David Gowan.

Watson Lake

Surrounded by granite boulders, Watson Lake is an ideal getaway from Arizona's summer heat, even though swimming is banned. Watson Lake is one of two reservoirs in the Granite Dells. Both reservoirs were formed in the 1900s after the Chino Valley Irrigation District built a dam on Granite Creek. In 1997, the City of Prescott bought 380 acres of land around the lake to be used as recreational land for visitors. The hiking trails that surround the lake are known for spring flower blooms. Some favorite activities are hiking, fishing, boating, kayaking, and camping along the shores. Fishing for rainbow trout, largemouth bass, and bluegills is very popular. In 2019, a fish ladder was created to help breed and re-habituate fish in the lake. The region is home to many bird species, such as golden eagles and canyon wrens. The Granite Dells near the lake is one of the most popular attractions in the region. Within the lake, there are granite boulders; decreased water levels over the years have left white rings around the lake.

Best Time to Visit: April to October

Pass/Permit/Fees: $3

Closest City or Town: Prescott

Physical Address: 3101 Watson Lake Park Rd, Prescott, AZ 86301

GPS Coordinates: 34.5915° N, 112.4216° W

Did You Know? Mercury mining caused Watson Lake to be polluted, so swimming is prohibited.

Butterfly Wonderland

Opened in 2013, the Butterfly Wonderland is the largest indoor butterfly conservatory in the country. The facility has a magnificent glass atrium that allows thousands of butterflies from around the world to fly around freely. Visitors can watch them fly around and drink nectar from the hundreds of flowers and plants. Butterflies are attracted to bright colors. Wearing white clothes is the best way to have a butterfly fly near or land on you.

In addition to the atrium, an immersive 3D theater provides education and an impressive video, "Flight of the Butterflies." Located within the Butterfly Wonderland is the "Butterfly Emergence Gallery," the most extensive in the country. This gallery allows visitors to see live chrysalis and the emerging of adult butterflies. Besides butterflies, there is a reptile and insect exhibition with varieties of reptiles and amphibians. There is also a large display of honeybees at work.

Best Time to Visit: Year-Round

Pass/Permit/Fees: $25 per person

Closest City or Town: Scottsdale

Physical Address: Butterfly Wonderland, 9500 East Vía de Ventura F100, Scottsdale, AZ 85256

GPS Coordinates: 33.5545° N, 111.8762° W

Did You Know? There is a vending machine that allows visitors to eat insects – including scorpion lollipops and coconut brittle mealworms.

MacDonald's Ranch

Located on 1,280 acres of land in the Sonoran Desert, MacDonald's Ranch allows visitors to ride horses and learn about the region's history. The ranch has been owned by the Richardson Family since 1956 and opened for western-style adventures in 1970 under the name Old MacDonald's Farm. The horse and cattle ranch, founded in the 1950s, has more than 36,000 acres of desert land in North Scottsdale. It was opened to visitors to allow children from the city to experience country life and see the natural surroundings.

In 1994, the farm was renamed MacDonald's Ranch. It is now a prime place for parties, gatherings, and cookouts in addition to horseback and stagecoach rides. MacDonald's Ranch hosts an annual pumpkin festival with a hay maze and pumpkin patch during the fall months. There are hayrides, a petting zoo, and pony rides for children, as well as lawn games for visitors to play.

Best Time to Visit: March to July

Pass/Permit/Fees: Free from November to September

Closest City or Town: Scottsdale

Physical Address: MacDonald's Ranch, 26540 N Scottsdale Rd, Scottsdale, AZ 85255

GPS Coordinates: 33.7249° N, 111.9273° W

Did You Know? The ranch allows for free horseback rides on birthdays.

McCormick-Stillman Railroad Park

The McCormick-Stillman Railroad Park is located on 40 acres of land and features a 15-inch gauge railroad, a railroad museum, and a Magma Arizona Railroad locomotive. In 1967 the Fowler McCormick family donated 100 acres of their ranch to the City of Scottsdale for people to enjoy. Nine years later, Guy Stillman built a 15-inch narrow gauge replica on the property, naming it the Paradise & Pacific Railroad. With financial support from the U.S. Marines and Senator Barry Goldwater, the McCormick Railroad Park opened in 1975. It was renamed the McCormick-Stillman Railroad Park in 1996.

The Paradise & Pacific Railroad now has 3,800 feet of track and another 1,400 feet of sidetracks. The Charro Carousel is another popular attraction, built in 1950 by The Allan Herschell Company. One of the most famous exhibitions is a Swiss railway clock, donated by the City of Interlaken, Switzerland, as a symbol of a partnership.

Best Time to Visit: March to May

Pass/Permit/Fees: Free to visit, $3 to ride the train and carousel

Closest City or Town: Scottsdale

Physical Address: McCormick-Stillman Railroad Park Parking, 7301 E. Indian Bend Road, Scottsdale, AZ 85250

GPS Coordinates: 33.5383° N, 111.9239° W

Did You Know? The land was originally used to raise purebred Arabian horses and Angus cattle.

McDowell Sonoran Preserve

The McDowell Sonoran Preserve is a protected and sustainable desert habitat that includes a network of hiking, biking, and horseback riding trails. It contains more than 30,500 acres and is the largest urban park in the United States. It is often called "the people's park" because of its importance to the community. One of the most popular trails is Tom's Thumb Trail, which stretches 4 miles. Many avid rock climbers come to McDowell to climb Tom's Thumb, Sven's Slab, and Granite Ballroom.

Through efforts by the McDowell Sonoran Conservancy, the preserve can maintain a thriving natural environment of animals, plants, and birds that visitors can see. McDowell has some of the best saguaro cacti in the Scottsdale area; Gambel's quails, geckos, and jackrabbits can also be seen. The preserve is separated into the Northern Region and Southern Region. Each region has restrooms, shaded ramadas, and water fountains.

Best Time to Visit: March to May

Pass/Permit/Fees: Free

Closest City or Town: Scottsdale

Physical Address: Gateway Trailhead - McDowell Sonoran Preserve, 18333 N Thompson Peak Pkwy, Scottsdale, AZ 85255

GPS Coordinates: 33.6495° N, 111.8589° W

Did You Know? Over 750,000 people visit the preserve each year.

Octane Raceway

The Octane Raceway allows visitors to speed up to 45 MPH, with tight corners and fly-downs. The 1/3-mile track is the only full-time indoor and outdoor track in the U.S. It starts indoors and moves into a sheltered outdoor section. The Octane Raceway is scored using the Fastest Lap format. The driver with the best lap time over 14 laps is the winner. Each ride is 4 miles of racing, lasting about 10 minutes. The electric karts have zero emissions, helping to keep the track clean and environmentally friendly. The Octane Raceway was opened in 2003, and in 2005 nine countries represented the first Indoor Kart World Championships.

In addition to the raceway, there is also a Velocity VR experience, a full arcade, and mini bowling within a 65,000-square-foot facility. The motion-tracking technology allows natural locomotion with cutting-edge VR gear. Some of the games' features are Sol Raiders, Zombie Outbreak Origins, and Singularity.

Best Time to Visit: Year-Round

Pass/Permit/Fees: $22 for one race

Closest City or Town: Scottsdale

Physical Address: Octane Raceway, 9119 E Talking Stick Way, Scottsdale, AZ 85250

GPS Coordinates: 33.5363° N, 111.8847° W

Did You Know? The Octane Raceway was formerly the F1 Race Factory. The name was changed in 2011.

OdySea Aquarium

The OdySea Aquarium is the largest in the Southwest; it holds 2,000,000 gallons of water and has more than 6,000 animals, representing 370 species, on display. There are over 65 exhibits in the aquarium, including seven touch pools and the world's only Russian sturgeon touch exhibit. The OdySea Voyager, the newest exhibit, offers the "world's only revolving aquarium experience." Guests sit in a stadium-seating-style theater with 46-foot viewing windows and travel in a "submarine" through a narrated 20-minute adventure in which they will encounter sea life varying from sea turtles and broad rays to giant lemon sharks. In addition to sea life, penguin and sloth interaction programs allow visitors to get up close with these animals.

OdySea Aquarium is located on the Arizona Boardwalk, hosting attractions, dining, and shopping. The outdoor exhibition area offers events for adults and families throughout the year.

Best Time to Visit: Year-Round

Pass/Permit/Fees: $35 for adults, $30 for students, $25 for children

Closest City or Town: Scottsdale

Physical Address: OdySea Aquarium, 9500 East Vía de Ventura Suite A-100, Scottsdale, AZ 85256

GPS Coordinates: 33.5558° N, 111.8769° W

Did You Know? The bathrooms even offer viewings of the shark habitats.

Old Town Scottsdale

The area comprising Old Town Scottsdale is full of 100 restaurants, bars, and nightclubs, along with hotels and resorts. This neighborhood was settled and developed in 1888 after Winfield Scott's purchase of 640 acres. Scott planted two olive trees that are still alive on 2nd Street. One of the iconic restaurants is the Sugar Bowl, which has been operating since 1958. With over 100 galleries, the area becomes especially popular during the Scottsdale ArtWalk.

The yearly Parada Del Sol has brought visitors into Old Town Scottsdale starting in 1951 and features the "West's Most Western Town." The Scottsdale Historical Museum, previously known as the "Little Red Schoolhouse," is now a must-see in Old Town, a great location to further learn about the history of Scottsdale.

Best Time to Visit: March to May

Pass/Permit/Fees: Free

Closest City or Town: Scottsdale

Physical Address: On the corner of E Indian School Rd and N Scottsdale Rd, Scottsdale, AZ 85251

GPS Coordinates: 33.4984° N, 111.9261° W

Did You Know? The original name of Scottsdale was "Orangedale."

Penske Racing Museum

The Penske Racing Museum displays a vast collection of cars, trophies, and other racing memorabilia. Penske Racing has over fifty years of racing experience and more than 400 major wins, including 17 Indianapolis 500-mile victories. Among the most memorable items in the museum is the replica of the Pontiac Catalina that Roger Penske drove at the 1963 Riverside 250. Other cars on display were driven by famed drivers Helio Castroneves and Gil de Ferran. Team Penske debuted at the 24 Hours of Daytona race in 1966.

The museum, which opened in 2002, has over 9,000 square feet of memorabilia, and the collection is regularly rotated. Eighteen cars are on display, which is a third of its total collection. An event room is available for private events and dinners in the museum. While the museum is located in Phoenix, the Penske Racing facility is located on 105 acres in Mooresville, North Carolina.

Best Time to Visit: Year-Round

Pass/Permit/Fees: Free

Closest City or Town: Scottsdale

Physical Address: Penske Racing Museum, 7125 E Chauncey Ln, Phoenix, AZ 85054

GPS Coordinates: 33.6509° N, 111.9266° W

Did You Know? Eleven of Penske's 13 Indy 500-winning cars are on display at the museum.

Pinnacle Peak Park

Pinnacle Peak Park stretches over 150 acres, and its trail offers some of the best views of Scottsdale. The trail is 1.7 miles to the peak, with 1,033 feet in elevation gain. It's not a loop trail, making the course nearly 4 miles in all. To reach the summit, visitors have to hike the "South Crack" and use a series of rock climbs to reach the summit. In addition to the trail, the park has rock climbing routes and picnic tables.

Pinnacle Peak is a granite summit that reaches 3,169 feet in elevation and is located in the park, which is part of the Sonoran Desert and features native Arizona plants and trees. A wide variety of wildlife is found there, including woodrats, mountain lions, coyotes, gray foxes, mule deer, rock squirrels, javelina, desert cottontail, desert tortoise, chuckwalla, desert spiny lizards, and several snake species. Historically, the Hohokam people hunted and gathered food in the area of Pinnacle Peak.

Best Time to Visit: March to May

Pass/Permit/Fees: Free

Closest City or Town: Scottsdale

Physical Address: Pinnacle Peak Park, 26802 N 102nd Way, Scottsdale, AZ 85262

GPS Coordinates: 33.7281° N, 111.8605° W

Did You Know? The peak was formed via a volcano nearly 23 million years ago.

Scottsdale ArtWalk

The Scottsdale ArtWalk is internationally known as an ideal event for art collectors. Because it's held in one of the most walking-friendly areas of Phoenix, cars are unnecessary for visiting the many restaurants and galleries. The ArtWalk was founded in 1975 and is popular throughout the Old Town Scottsdale Art District; the area is full of statues, fountains, courtyards, and restaurants. Every Thursday, all galleries belonging to the Scottsdale Gallery Association (SGA) open their doors to the public. Trolleys and horse-drawn carriages offer excellent transportation between the galleries.

Some of the top restaurants in the city are located in the ArtWalk area. One of the most popular events hosted by Scottsdale ArtWalk is the Gold Palette, which offers special series throughout the year, including the famed season kickoff and chocolate event in October. Located in the ArtWalk are two museums that also host extended hours on the ArtWalk night.

Best Time to Visit: March to May, every Thursday

Pass/Permit/Fees: Free

Closest City or Town: Scottsdale

Physical Address: ArtWalk, E Main St, Scottsdale, AZ 85251

GPS Coordinates: 33.4933° N, 111.9244° W

Did You Know? More than 100 galleries are open every Thursday during ArtWalk.

Scottsdale Civic Center Mall

This Civic Center Mall, located outside the Arts District of Scottsdale, offers an array of activities and sights. It's not a shopping mall but instead features three acres of pristine public space in the heart of downtown. The area began in the early 1970s as part of the neighborhood redevelopment program. The overall program included a performing arts center, a hotel, restaurants, and a shopping center.

The mall offers a great way to spend the day visiting attractions, including the City Hall and Civic Center Library. Other popular spots to visit within the mall are the LOVE Sculpture, where many visitors enjoy having their photos taken, an outdoor amphitheater, fountains, museums, and a lagoon. The Civic Center offers some of the best views of Camelback Mountain, especially near sunset.

Best Time to Visit: March to May

Pass/Permit/Fees: Free

Closest City or Town: Scottsdale

Physical Address: Scottsdale Museum of Contemporary Art is at the heart of the Mall at 7374 E 2nd St, Scottsdale, AZ 85251.

GPS Coordinates: 33.4928° N, 111.9217° W

Did You Know? A $27.3 million renovation of the mall has begun that will include a permanent outdoor stage for live music and theater performances, several busker platforms, and a community plaza for outdoor events.

Scottsdale Fashion Square

The Fashion Square in Scottsdale has over 200 stores, restaurants, and a movie theater. This is the largest shopping mall in all of Arizona and is among the top 30 largest malls in the country. In the 1930s and 1940s, the land that the mall currently sits on was not deemed valuable. Harry Lenart bought 40 acres at an undisclosed price and opened a small shopping center with four stores in 1959.

Edward L. Varney Associates designed a three-floor open-air structure in 1961 to compete with other malls in Scottsdale, including an expansion that doubled the square footage of the original mall. In 1982, the owners of the Scottsdale Fashion Square and the Camelview Plaza connected the two malls via a two-story retail bridge. Following multiple expansions, the Scottsdale Fashion Square has over 225 stores and 17 floors.

Best Time to Visit: Year-Round

Pass/Permit/Fees: Free

Closest City or Town: Scottsdale

Physical Address: Scottsdale Fashion Square, 7014 E Camelback Rd, Scottsdale, AZ 85251

GPS Coordinates: 33.5028° N, 111.9293° W

Did You Know? The Scottsdale Fashion Square contains over 2 million square feet and attracts about 11 million visitors a year.

Scottsdale Historical Museum

This museum is now operating out of the Little Red Schoolhouse. Located in the Old Town of Scottsdale, the museum highlights the history and early settlers of the Scottsdale region. In 1896, Chaplin Winfield Scott saw the need for a school and educational system for local children. Mrs. Blount, whose husband was the principal of the Phoenix School, taught eight children at her home until the townspeople raised funds for a 16x18-foot wood building that opened with fourteen students. The first teacher, Hattie Green, was paid 45 dollars a month. The present Little Red Schoolhouse opened in 1909. The school taught students in Grades 1 through 8 until 1928. The original school was going to be destroyed in 1968, but the Scottsdale Historical Society was created to save the building. In 1991 the Historical Society opened the old school as the Historical Museum, displaying old photographs and a classroom with artifacts from 1910. This museum is a great way to learn about early Scottsdale history and see photos of the children who attended the Little Red Schoolhouse.

Best Time to Visit: March to June

Pass/Permit/Fees: Free

Closest City or Town: Scottsdale

Physical Address: Scottsdale Historical Museum, 7333 E Scottsdale Mall, Scottsdale, AZ 85251

GPS Coordinates: 33.4929° N, 111.9257° W

Did You Know? Visitors can ring the old school bell.

Scottsdale Museum of Contemporary Art

Located in the Old Town District of Scottsdale, the art museum is home to modern artwork, design, and architecture. This is the only museum in Arizona that is dedicated to contemporary works of art, with over 2,000 pieces in its collection. The museum has four galleries that display its permanent collection and rotating shows. It was created in 1988 and officially opened in February 1999. The building, which previously housed a movie theater, was redesigned by architect Will Bruder

One of its most famous works is "Knight Rise," in James Turrell's "Skyspace" series. "Knight Rise" allows visitors to experience the changing light of the desert sky. Some of the other famed artists include Yves Klein, Russel Wright, and Josef Albers. Works by living artists Kara Walker and William Wegmans are permanently on display. The museum also hosts many events, including film and art festivals and educational programs about art, performances, and science.

Best Time to Visit: Year-Round

Pass/Permit/Fees: $12

Closest City or Town: Scottsdale

Physical Address: Scottsdale Museum of Contemporary Art, E 2nd St, Scottsdale, AZ

GPS Coordinates: 33.4916° N and 111.9251° W.

Did You Know? The museum is surrounded by a gorgeous city park that features fountains and public sculptures.

Scottsdale Wine Trail

Five wineries that are within walking distance of downtown Scottsdale — the Aridus Wine Company, Carlson Creek, LDV Winery, Merkin Vineyards, and Salvatore Vineyards — collaborate to create the Scottsdale Wine Trail. The five wineries are located within the Art, 5th Ave Shopping, and Old Town District. Each winery has tailored tasting and menus for the wine trail. The wineries are surrounded by local shops, restaurants, and art galleries, so the trail helps increase the local economy. The Downtown Trolley also runs through the trail – an excellent option for those who don't want to walk it. The wine trail was founded in 2016 to help promote the wine industry in the region. Visitors receive a "Wine Passport" that entitles them to a discount on the wine tasting at each winery they visit. The Scottsdale Wine Trail is a great way to experience Arizona wine without needing to drive far distances. The trail annually offers two special events: the Shamrocks & Shenanigans Wine Scavenger Hunt in March and the Scottsdazzle Santa Wine Around in December.

Best Time to Visit: March to May

Pass/Permit/Fees: Free to visit, but wine prices will vary

Closest City or Town: Scottsdale

Physical Address: Scottsdale Wine Trail, 7134 E Stetson Dr B-110, Scottsdale, AZ 85251

GPS Coordinates: 33.4994° N, 111.9279° W

Did You Know? 75% of grapes grown in Arizona come from the Wilcox area.

Southwest Wildlife Conservation Center

This sanctuary is devoted to rescuing wild animals that have been injured, orphaned, or abandoned. The Southwest Wildlife Conservation Center works to rehabilitate and release animals back into the wild. Linda Searles, who founded the center, rescued an orphaned coyote pup in the early 1990s. She purchased 10 acres of land in Scottsdale, planted trees to create shade, and built enclosures. The orphaned coyote pup, Don, lived at the center for more than 18 years. Now one of the country's largest conservation centers, the center provides sanctuary for animals that cannot be released to live healthy and happy lives. An impressive 70 percent of all animals that have come into the center have been released into the wild. Perhaps the center's most significant accomplishment is the recovery of the endangered Mexican gray wolf. Southwest Center gives education tours to help the public learn about conservation.

Best Time to Visit: Year-Round

Pass/Permit/Fees: Tours by appointment only, call (480) 471-9109

Closest City or Town: Scottsdale

Physical Address: Southwest Wildlife Conservation Center, 27026 N 156th St, Scottsdale, AZ 85262

GPS Coordinates: 33.7314° N, 111.7489° W

Did You Know? This center is a non-profit organization funded solely through private donations, fundraising, and grants and operated by a small full-time staff and a large group of dedicated volunteers.

Taliesin West

When famed architect Frank Lloyd Wright's health began to decline, his doctors recommended spending the winters in a warmer location than harsh Wisconsin, where he had built his original Taliesin estate. In 1937, Wright bought a plot of desert land, and he and his students lived in tents on the property while building a house with local materials. The house is made with rocks, wood, and concrete often referred to as "desert masonry." This design helps keep the house cool during intense Arizona summers. Wright felt that it was necessary to incorporate native Arizona colors, along with native rocks and lumber.

Many of Wright's most famous designs were created in this house, including the Guggenheim Museum in New York City and the Grady Gammage Auditorium in Arizona. Wright lived at Taliesin West during the winters for nearly 20 years. In 2008, the Taliesin West house and nine other Wright properties were given World Heritage status.

Best Time to Visit: Year-round

Pass/Permit/Fees: $40 for adults, $30 for students

Closest City or Town: Scottsdale

Physical Address: Taliesin West, 12621 N Frank Lloyd Wright Blvd, Scottsdale, AZ 85259

GPS Coordinates: 33.6064° N, 111.8452° W

Did You Know? Taliesin was the great Chief of Bards, a poet and advisor of kings, in Welsh legend.

Western Spirit: Scottsdale's Museum of the West

Ranked one of the best Western museums in the country, the Western Spirit Museum highlights the art, culture, and history of 19 different states. It contains 43,000 square feet, with two stories of exhibitions and artwork. There are eight exhibit spaces, a sculpture courtyard, a 135-seat multi-sensory and multimedia theater, and a gift shop. Heritage Hall presents photos and bios of important Westerners such as Sandra Day O'Connor, the first woman Supreme Court justice; Billy the Kid, notorious thief and gunfighter; and Bill Gates, founder of Microsoft. Some of the most popular exhibits include "The Story of Lewis & Clark," featuring 100 paintings by Charles Fritz of the pair's famous expedition. The A.P. Hays "Sport of the West Collection" features saddles, revolvers, and spurs, all iconic symbols of Western American history. The mission of the museum is to educate about the history of Western American and Native American history.

Best Time to Visit: Year-Round

Pass/Permit/Fees: $13 per adult, $8 per child

Closest City or Town: Scottsdale

Physical Address: Western Spirit, 3830 N Marshall Way, Scottsdale, AZ 85251

GPS Coordinates: 33.4924° N and 111.9307° W

Did You Know? This museum is an affiliate of the Smithsonian Institution.

Xeriscape Garden

One of Scottsdale's best-kept secrets is the Xeriscape Gardena, a hidden desert oasis that is full of cacti, desert trees, and beautiful flowers. A xeriscape garden is a type of landscaping that requires little irrigation and other maintenance, and these gardens are very popular in arid regions. It thrives without needing the amount of water that a traditional garden would.

Christine Ten Eyck designed the garden as a water conservatory. A rusty steel water vessel serves as a focal point of the garden, with the inscription, "The frog does not drink up the pond in which he lives." The garden helps conceal a 5.5-million-gallon reservoir from the Chaparral Water Treatment Plant. There are over 7,000 plants and 200 different species of plants in the garden. Signage and an interactive plant guide teach park visitors about low-water-use plants and trees, water harvesting, and other tips for caring for the desert landscape

Best Time to Visit: March to May

Pass/Permit/Fees: Free

Closest City or Town: Scottsdale

Physical Address: Xeriscape Garden, 5401 N Hayden Rd, Scottsdale, AZ 85250

GPS Coordinates: 33.5151° N, 111.9077° W

Did You Know? Located in Scottsdale's Chaparral Park and hidden from the street, the Xeriscape Garden is nestled behind the dog park and baseball fields.

86

Airport Mesa

The Airport Mesa is a favorite hike that is known for views of the Sedona region and being a famed vortex site. The walk is 3.3 miles round trip and is often called "a cathedral without walls" because of the tall red rock walls. From the top of the mesa, hikers can see the iconic Bell Rock and Courthouse Butte in the distance. Many hikers will visit the Airport Mesa for its spiritual vortex. People claim to feel healing powers, and it's common to see people meditating among the rocks. The series of vortices in Sedona is powerful due to the swirling and near cosmic forces radiating from the red rocks.

Three popular festivals are held here each year: the Sedona Yoga Festival, Red Rocks Music Festival, and Sedona Hummingbird Festival. One of the reasons for Airport Mesa's popularity is its proximity to Sedona, making it easy for visitors to reach the trails. Hiking the courses is best in the early morning or late at night to avoid the intense Arizona summer heat.

Best Time to Visit: February to May

Pass/Permit/Fees: Free

Closest City or Town: Sedona

Physical Address: Airport Mesa Vortex, 483 Airport Rd, Sedona, AZ 86336

GPS Coordinates: 34.8552° N, 111.7821° W

Did You Know? The Spanish word "mesa" means "table," and it's commonly used for a mountain that has a flat top.

Amitabha Stupa and Peace Park

Located in Sedona, this spiritual hub is visited by people from around the world to experience the spiritual pull of the area. Created in 2004, this peaceful park is nestled among pinion and juniper pines with crimson spires surrounding the area. Located at the base of Thunder Mountain, this land was also deemed holy by the Native Americans who previously lived in this region. The short trail leads visitors to the 36-foot Amitabha Stupa and the smaller Tara Stupa for praying and meditation. A stupa is a dome-shaped structure commonly used in Buddhism as a place to pray and meditate. The stupa at Peace Park is bronze, and its caretakers say it is filled with hundreds of millions of peace prayers and sacred relics. The White Tara stupa is 6 feet tall and represents a female Buddha; this statue is said to embody long life and compassion to those who pray there. Peace Park is filled with prayer flags, wooden boards for sitting and meditating, and a medicine wheel. The stupas are situated on pristine Sedona land and offer unobstructed views of Sedona and the iconic red rock mountains of the region.

Best Time to Visit: March to June

Pass/Permit/Fees: Free

Closest City or Town: Sedona

Physical Address: Amitabha Stupa and Peace Park, 2650 Pueblo Dr, Sedona, AZ 86336

GPS Coordinates: 34.8755° N and 111.8104° W

Did You Know? This is the only stupa in Arizona.

Bell Rock

Bell Rock reaches an elevation just short of 5,000 feet (4,919ft) and can take 2-3 hours for hikers to reach. There is a moderate trail to the plateau, but a steep, unmarked trail awaits those wanting to reach the summit. Bell Rock is composed of red and brown sedimentary rock that lays horizontally and is quite a sight to see for anyone visiting the Sedona area.

The Bell Rock Pathway to the plateau is a 3.6-mile hike that features views of Courthouse Butte and other landmarks along the way, including the Bell Rock Vortex- known for its meditative powers. An observation deck is to the west of Bell Rock, and a steeper trail to the summit is on the east side. The trail starts at the Courthouse Vista parking lot. Follow signs for Bell Rock Climb.

Best Time to Visit: May to October

Pass/Permit/Fees: $5 for daily passes

Closest City or Town: Sedona

Physical Address: Courthouse Vista Visitor Kiosk, AZ-79 S, Sedona, Arizona 86336

GPS Coordinates: 34.8003° N, 111.7733° W

Did You Know? Despite being a steep uphill hike, this trail is one of the best in Sedona for families with young children.

Boynton Canyon

Boynton Canyon is one of the most beautiful box canyons in all of Arizona Red Rock Country. This canyon has gained popularity because of its site of spiritual energy – a vortex. The vortex at Boynton Canyon is said to be a site of balance. The ancient Sinagua ruins can be seen in the canyon. The hike takes around 2 hours round-trip and is rated easy. A detour, the 0.2 mile Boynton Vista Trail, offers incredible views of the region and a prominent rock formation known as the Kachina Woman. Visitors with good eyesight may be able to make out some cliff-dwelling ruins hidden in the canyon walls. Visitors can walk through the canyon floor, a favorite among hikers because it is shaded with trees and tends to be cooler in temperature. Because the trail has an elevation change of only 500 feet, it is very popular among visitors who want to see Sedona's iconic red rocks. Wildlife is abundant along the trail, including lizards, birds, and insects.

Best Time to Visit: March to May

Pass/Permit/Fees: Parking fee required

Closest City or Town: Sedona

Physical Address: Meeting Village at Enchantment Resort, 525 Boynton Canyon Rd, Sedona, AZ 86336, is one mile away from the vortex.

GPS Coordinates: 34.9118° N, 111.8482° W

Did You Know? Boynton Canyon is one of four main vortices in the Sedona region.

Cathedral Rock

This is one of the most popular trails around Sedona. It only measures one mile, but it can be difficult because of its elevation gain of 608 feet. The trail takes hikers between the towering buttes of red striped sandstone. Four main rock formations can be seen. These sandstone buttes within the Coconino National Forest were formed by water and wind erosion over millions of years.

Oak Creek runs alongside Cathedral Rock, and this area was often called "Red Rock Crossing" by the Navajo and Hopi Native Americans. This region is considered to be sacred as the home of gods and the birthplace of men and women, according to the local Native Americans. The top of Cathedral Rock offers views of the landscape in Coconino National Forest. One of the reasons for the popularity is the vortex that many believe is present here. People claim that the vortices release feminine energy and leave visitors feeling more creative and well-rested.

Best Time to Visit: March to May; October to November

Pass/Permit/Fees: $5 per car

Closest City or Town: Sedona

Physical Address: Cathedral Rock Trailhead, Back O Beyond Rd., Sedona, AZ 86351

GPS Coordinates: 34.8200° N, 111.7932° W

Did You Know? Cathedral Rock was given that name because it resembles a grand cathedral.

Slide Rock State Park

This park in the Coconino National Forest gets its name from the natural water slide located along the bed of Oak Creek. This land was first developed in 1907 by Frank L. Pendley, and he was granted title to it under the Homestead Act of 1910. Pendley developed an irrigation system and planted an orchard in 1912. The canyon road was built in 1914 and paved in 1938, greatly encouraging recreational use of the canyon, leading Pendley to build rustic cabins to cater to vacationers and sightseers. It is one of the last remaining homesteads and an excellent example of early agricultural development. The state purchased the 43-acre site in 1985 to create the park. Some of the most popular trails in the park are Pendley Homestead Trail, Slide Rock Route, and Clifftop Nature Trail. Algae on the rocks add to their slipperiness. Besides the natural rockslide, swimming and hiking are popular activities. This park shares similarities with other Sedona rocks, and the vibrant red hues stand out among the blue water of Oak Creek.

Best Time to Visit: March to June

Pass/Permit/Fees: $20 per vehicles

Closest City or Town: Sedona

Physical Address: Slide Rock State Park, 6871 AZ-89A, Sedona, AZ 86336

GPS Coordinates: 34.9436° N, 111.7529° W

Did You Know? The irrigation system installed more than a century ago is still operating.

Tlaquepaque Arts and Shopping Village

The Tlaquepaque Village is based on a city in Mexico known for its bright culture. Located in the shade of sycamore trees, Tlaquepaque translates to "best of everything." Founded in the 1970s, the space originally housed an artist community. It is filled with vine-covered stucco walls, cobbled walkways, and archways, and the architecture gives the feeling that the village has been around for centuries.

Tlaquepaque Village is home to more than 50 shops and galleries, many of which are filled with traditional Western and Native American art. Artists use the village as a place of inspiration, and visitors can watch many of them creating their work. Among the most popular artworks are bronze sculptures, ceramics, and blown glass pieces, many inspired by the nature of Sedona and Arizona. The chapel in the village offers couples the chance to get married among sycamore trees, water fountains, and ivy-covered buildings.

Best Time to Visit: March to May

Pass/Permit/Fees: Free

Closest City or Town: Sedona

Physical Address: Tlaquepaque Arts and Shopping Village, 336 AZ-179, Sedona, AZ 86336

GPS Coordinates: 34.862515° N, 111.7637955° W

Did You Know? Tlaquepaque is pronounced T-lockey-pockey.

Big Surf Water Park

Big Surf Water Park is a 20-acre site that has over a dozen water slides and other rides. The Waikiki Beach Wave pool (named after the beach in Hawaii) holds 2.5 gallons of water and was deemed an American Society of Mechanical Engineering Historic Landmark for being "the first inland surfing facility in North America." The park, which opened in 1969, is the oldest wave pool in the United States. World champion surfer Fred Hemmings was hired as a consultant and a featured surfer.

The Big Surf Water Park has a range of other water features, including the Hurricane, Black Hole, White Serpentine, Kilauea Cove, and Tornado Twister water slides. A favorite among visitors is the 300-foot Maua Kea Zip Line that stretches over the wave pool. Big Surf also features three dedicated areas for children. The park has grassy hills and sidewalks with flowing water to cool its sidewalks from the intense heat of Arizona.

Best Time to Visit: May to August

Pass/Permit/Fees: $33.95 per adult, $28.95 per child

Closest City or Town: Tempe

Physical Address: Big Surf, 1500 N McClintock Dr, Tempe, AZ 85281

GPS Coordinates: 33.4457° N, 111.9119° W

Did You Know? Pink Floyd performed at Big Surf in 1972.

Grady Gammage Memorial Auditorium

This auditorium, on the Arizona State University campus, is a multipurpose performing arts center that's listed on the National Register of Historic Places. It was named for former ASU President Grady Gammage and is one of the last public commissions of famed architect Frank Lloyd Wright. After the roof collapsed in the previous auditorium, Gammage asked his friend Wright to design the auditorium. Wright based the design on that of an opera house in Baghdad that was never built. Construction began in 1957, and both Gammage and Wright died in 1959, five years before the official opening.

The $2.46 million building stands 80 feet high and has two pedestrian bridges. In addition to musical and dramatic performances, the auditorium has been the site of Arizona Senator Barry Goldwater's funeral and a 2004 presidential debate. The auditorium contains three galleries that feature paintings and photography by local Arizona artists.

Best Time to Visit: Year-Round

Pass/Permit/Fees: Ticket prices vary per show

Closest City or Town: Tempe

Physical Address: Grady Gammage Memorial Auditorium, 1200 S Forest Ave, Tempe, AZ 85281

GPS Coordinates: 33.4163° N, 111.9380° W

Did You Know? This auditorium is the only public building in Arizona that was designed by Frank Lloyd Wright.

Lake Mead National Recreation Area

Located on the western border of Arizona, Lake Mead was the country's first national recreation area. After the construction of the Hoover Dam began in 1931, a reservoir was created by damming the Colorado River. This reservoir became Lake Mead, named after the commissioner of the Bureau of Reclamation at the time. With recent droughts, the lake's water has decreased, and the encircling white layer of rock shows previous water level heights. The region encompasses over 1.5 million acres of land, including mountains, canyons, and two lakes. Lake Mead Recreation Area is located within three of the four desert ecosystems in the entire United States: the Mojave, the Great Basin, and the Sonoran Desert. The lake is nestled between two mountain ranges, the River and Muddy Mountains, which allow for hiking and climbing. With the vast amount of land, there are multiple ways to enjoy the region: boating, hiking, camping, and fishing. Boaters can find cliffs and beaches on the shores surrounding the lake.

Best Time to Visit: May to September

Pass/Permit/Fees: Seven-day passes are $25 per vehicle, $20 per motorcycle, and $15 per bicycle or pedestrian

Closest City or Town: Temple Bar Marina

Physical Address: Temple Bar Campground, Campgrounds Rd., Temple Bar Marina, AZ 86443

GPS Coordinates: 36.1551° N, 114.4559° W

Did You Know? There are at least two crashed planes at the bottom of Lake Mead.

96

White Mesa Arch

The White Mesa Arch is located near the Tonalea region of Arizona within the Navajo reservation. The half-mile hike to the arch takes around 30 minutes. The sandy clay roads are ideal for high clearance 4x4 vehicles if you make sure that you drive only on trails. The arch is 53 feet wide and 84 feet tall, with layers of white limestone and red, white, yellow, and pink sandstone. Years of erosion created the thick layers of cross-bedded sandstone from windblown sand dunes formed in that ancient desert, which is the largest known sand desert in the world's history. The best times to visit the arch is during sunrise or sunset when it has a red glow. The Navajo Stand Rock and Margaret Arch are two other rock formations located close to the White Mesa Arch. This arch offers an excellent location for learning about the rock formations of sand and limestone. Visitors should not climb or walk on the arch.

Best Time to Visit: March to May

Pass/Permit/Fees: Free

Closest City or Town: Tonalea

Physical Address: Continue on Indian Route 6260, Tonalea, AZ 86044 for 1.7 miles and then turn right onto the dirt road to reach the Mesa. The GPS coordinates will lead you to an open area to park and see the Mesa.

GPS Coordinates: 36.4729° N, 110.9613° W

Did You Know? Caution is required because there are steep drop-offs and unfenced overlooks along the trail.

Catalina State Park

This popular state park is located at the base of the Santa Catalina Mountains and is famous for the 5,000 saguaros and desert plants. In addition to the desert plants, more than 150 species of native animals live in the park, which contains more than 5,500 acres of foothills and canyons for hiking. Among the most popular hiking trails in the park are the Romero Ruin Trail, Nature Trail, and Romero Canyon Trail. Some of these trails connect to other courses in the Coronado National.

The park was officially established in 1974 and has been designated as an Important Birding Area by the Audubon Society. Some of the most significant birds are the Rufous-winged sparrow and the yellow-billed cuckoo. People have been living in the region since 5000 BCE, beginning with the Hohokam people, who built pueblos and adobes into the rocks. Visitors from all over the country come to visit Catalina State Park for camping, horseback riding, and hiking.

Best Time to Visit: March to May

Pass/Permit/Fees: $7 per day

Closest City or Town: Tucson

Physical Address: Catalina State Park, 11570 N Oracle Rd, Tucson, AZ 85737

GPS Coordinates: 32.4364° N, 110.9096° W

Did You Know? The park reaches a peak elevation of 2,854 ft.

Colossal Cave Mountain Park

With over 3.5 miles of passageways and an average internal temperature of 70 degrees, the Colossal Cave system is a favorite among people looking to avoid the summer heat. It is classified as an ancient karst cave and is a dry cave, meaning that the geological formations are dead and do not grow. Water deposits created the limestone formations, but the water source disappeared, resulting in the cave's "death."

According to geologists, the Colossal Cave is a newer cave system with organic material that became the limestone seen today in the cave. This cave is one of the largest "dry" caves in North America. In January 1879, Solomon Lick was searching for stray cattle when he discovered an entrance to the cave, believing it to be an old mine. The Colossal Cave Mountain Park is part of a network of other caves. The park also hosts the La Posta Quemada Ranch Museum and multiple horse-riding trails.

Best Time to Visit: Year-Round

Pass/Permit/Fees: $18 adults, $9 children

Closest City or Town: Tucson

Physical Address: Colossal Cave Mountain Park, 16721 E Old Spanish Trail, Vail, AZ 85641

GPS Coordinates: 32.06508° N, 110.630914° W

Did You Know? The Hohokam, Sobaipuri, and Apache Indians lived in the Colossal Cave system from 900 to 1450 AD.

El Presidio Historic District

This historic district is located on the old City of Tucson site when it was a military fort in 1775. The 12-foot-high walls were made of 3-inch-thick adobe brick. The Presidio San Agustin del Tucson Museum, a reconstruction of the original Tucson Presidio, is now home to many artifacts of the period. Before the Spanish fort was built, the land was occupied by a Native American community. There is evidence of a 2,000year-old prehistoric pit house. Among the most popular sights are the original 150-year-old Sonoran row houses.

The historic district city block is home to art galleries and shops. These are the longest-inhabited buildings in all of Tucson, built in 1850 and over the remains of the original Presidio wall. The Tucson Museum of Art and Historic Block, founded in 1924, has some of the most extensive collections of Native American, Latin American, and American West art pieces in the city.

Best Time to Visit: March to May

Pass/Permit/Fees: Free

Closest City or Town: Tucson

Physical Address: Presidio San Agustín del Tucson Museum, 196 N Court Ave, Tucson, AZ 85701

GPS Coordinates: 32.2256° N, 110.9762° W

Did You Know? Tucson was the first city to receive the UNESCO City of Gastronomy designation.

International Wildlife Museum

The International Wildlife Museum was founded in 1988 by C.J McElroy as an educational project of the Safari Club International Foundation. The museum has animals on displays that mimic their natural habitat, including a rock display with mountain goats. Many of the collections were donated by government agencies, captive breeding programs, and rehabilitation centers from around the country, and several are more than 100 years old.

The museum was built to look like a fort. The taxidermized animals are used for education about habitats and legal game hunting. Among the most popular exhibits display are "Big Terror," which includes a tiger killed in India in 1969 and a rhinoceros killed by President Theodore Roosevelt. The Sensory Safari is a facility where visitors are encouraged to learn about the animals via touch and feel. The museum hosts workshops and festivals throughout the year to celebrate animals and natural events from around the world.

Best Time to Visit: March to May

Pass/Permit/Fees: $9 adults, $7 children

Closest City or Town: Tucson

Physical Address: International Wildlife Museum, 4800 West Gates Pass, Boulevard, Tucson, AZ 85745

GPS Coordinates: 32.2346° N, 111.0670° W

Did You Know? There are over 400 species of birds, insects, and mammals from around the world on display.

Mission San Xavier del Bac

A registered National Historic Landmark, the San Xavier Mission was founded as a Catholic mission in 1692 by Father Eusebio Francisco Kino. Construction of the original mission began in 1700. The "del Bac" portion of its name comes from the Tohono O'odham people, meaning "place where water appears." The mission is located atop a natural spring. It is one of the only churches still run by the Franciscans, and the Franciscan Sisters of Christian Charity have taught there since 1872. Located behind the church is a grotto hill, with a statue of Lourdes.

Mission San Xavier del Bac is the oldest European structure in Arizona and still has its original sculpture and mural paintings. In 1939 lightning struck the west tower, burning it down. It was rebuilt in 2007, using threaded fiberglass-reinforced rods to protect from lightning. Extensive preservation work began in 1992 and continues. The mission's interior is now in much of its original state, with brilliant colors in complex designs.

Best Time to Visit: Year-Round

Pass/Permit/Fees: Free

Closest City or Town: Tucson

Physical Address: Mission San Xavier del Bac, 1950 W San Xavier Rd, Tucson, AZ 85746

GPS Coordinates: 32.1070° N, 111.0088° W

Did You Know? The mission's nickname is "the White Dove Desert."

Mount Lemmon Scenic Byway

Known as one of Arizona's most scenic drives, the byway takes drivers up Mount Lemmon, the highest peak in the Santa Catalina Mountain Range. The mountain is surrounded by the Coronado National Forest, which has been afflicted by wildfires in recent years. The drive, also called Catalina Highway or the Sky Island Scenic byway, is about 27 miles one way and climbs up over 9,000 feet in elevation. The drive takes a minimum of two hours to travel.

Visitors will see many types of vegetation, from thick forest at the top to desert terrain at the base. There are also many different rock formations. Rest areas along the drive offer 180-degree views of the regions below, including the famous Windy Point, an overlook of the Tucson Valley below. The top of Mount Lemmon hosts a ski valley. The byway is open all year, but spring and summer are the best times to visit.

Best Time to Visit: March to September

Pass/Permit/Fees: $5 per vehicle

Closest City or Town: Tucson

Physical Address: Use the Bug Spring Trailhead entrance to find the start of the byway at Catalina Hwy, Mt. Lemmon, AZ 85619

GPS Coordinates: 32.4434° N, -110.7881° W

Did You Know? The temperature difference between the base and top can be over 30 degrees.

Pima Air and Space Museum

The Pima Air and Space Museum was founded to celebrate the 25th anniversary of the United States Air Force. It opened to the public in 1976 with 35 planes on display. There are now more than 400 aircraft spread over 80 acres.

Among the most famous planes on display are a Boeing 777, Boeing B-17 Flying Fortress, Boeing B-29 Superfortress, Consolidated B-24 Liberator, Convair B-36J Peacemaker, English Electric Lightning, Lockheed SR-71 Blackbird, Martin PBM Mariner, North American F-107, Aero Spacelines Super Guppy, Boeing 747-100, Boeing 787, and a Douglas DC-10. In 2021, the museum constructed the Tucson Military Vehicle Museum, which contains mostly land vehicles, including 50 that were donated by London's Imperial War Museum. The museum is also home to the Arizona Aviation Hall of Fame.

Best Time to Visit: Year-Round

Pass/Permit/Fees: $16.50 for adults, $10 for children

Closest City or Town: Tucson

Physical Address: Pima Air and Space Museum, 6000 E Valencia Rd, Tucson, AZ 85756

GPS Coordinates: 32.1390° N, 110.8687° W

Did You Know? This is one of the world's largest non-government-funded aerospace museums.

Reid Park Zoo

Located in Tucson, the Reid Park Zoo was founded in 1967 on 24 acres of land owned by the city. In 1965, park and recreation director Gene Reid created a fledgling zoo showcasing birds and guinea fowl. Reid added more animals to the grounds the following year, including a Prairie dog exhibition and an Asian elephant. The Reid Park Zoo is owned by the City of Tucson and a non-profit Reid Park Zoological Society.

The zoo is located in a 131-acre park that also has a baseball stadium, performance center, and public pool. Among the most popular animals are elephants, bears, anteaters, otters, and rhinos. A medical facility was created in partnership with the University of Arizona Cancer Center to help treat animals that suffer from cancer. With over 500,000 visitors each year, the zoo is one of the most popular attractions in Tucson. In addition to the animals, the zoo features a carousel and miniature train.

Best Time to Visit: March to May – animals most active in the morning hours

Pass/Permit/Fees: $10.50 adult

Closest City or Town: Tucson

Physical Address: Reid Park Zoo, 3400 E Zoo Ct, Tucson, AZ 85716

GPS Coordinates: 32.2099° N, 110.9207° W

Did You Know? The Reid Park Zoo has more than 500 animals living in four habitat zones and an aviary.

Saguaro National Park

If you're looking for desert scenery and some of the most enormous cacti in the United States, visit Saguaro National Park, named after the saguaro cactus that grows in the region. Some of the oldest rocks in the park were formed nearly 1.7 billion years ago, including 1.4-billion-year-old granites. In 1961, President John F. Kennedy added 16,000 acres of protected land, including Saguaro National Park. The park covers nearly 92,000 acres of land with two districts. The eastern side, Rincon Mountain District, has a smaller number of cacti, but you can see the mountains. The Tucson Mountain District offers cacti on the western side and 165 miles of trails for hiking and paved roads allowing bicycling and horseback riding. The area is home to nearly 1.8 million saguaro cacti, which can grow up to 60 feet high and weigh about 4,800 pounds. There are 30 different species of animals in the park, including cougars, javelina, and an endangered lesser long-nosed bat.

Best Time to Visit: October to April

Pass/Permit/Fees: Seven-day passes are $14 for vehicles, $7 for bikes or motorcycles

Closest City or Town: Tucson

Physical Address: Saguaro National Park Tucson Mountain District Visitor Center, 2700 N Kinney Rd., Tucson, AZ 85743

GPS Coordinates: 32.2967° N, 111.1666° W

Did You Know? Saguaro cactus can live up to 200 years under the right conditions.

Seven Falls

Located in the Bear Canyon at the Catalina Foothills, these falls are made up of limestone rocks. The hike to reach Seven Falls is one of the most popular trails in the Tucson region. For those who do not want to hike, a tram can take visitors to the trailhead; this makes the trail only three to four miles rather than nine miles. The hike to reach Seven Falls passes through rivers and creeks, so it's a good idea to wear water shoes during the trek. During the rainy season, the water to the falls can be waist-high. The waterfall is more enjoyable in the spring when the water flow is at its most powerful. The limestone and granite rocks of the area offer various colors, and there are plants surrounding the falls. Many small waterfalls appear during the high-flowing seasons because the water forms pools at the falls' base. This is ideal for hikers looking to cool off, especially during the summer. The water flow in the area allows vegetation to grow, unlike other Bear Canyon areas.

Best Time to Visit: March to May

Pass/Permit/Fees: $5 per vehicle

Closest City or Town: Tucson

Physical Address: Seven Falls, Bear Canyon Trail, Tucson, AZ 85749

GPS Coordinates: 32.3276° N, 110.7709° W

Did You Know? Exploring the region, you will find native cactus and even the Costa hummingbird, which is native to this area and Mexico.

St. Augustine Cathedral

The first Cathedral of Saint Augustine was opened in 1858 in a two-room house that was donated by parishioners. Father Donato Rogieri became the pastor in the early 1860s. After each Sunday service, he and his parishioners would collect adobe bricks and stack them at the church site to build new walls. The structure was completed in 1868. The church was rebuilt in 1897, but the spires called for in the original plans were never completed. A 1928 renovation, inspired by the Cathedral of Querétaro in Mexico, created its present Mexican baroque design with a façade of cast stone. The structure that stands today was created by a restoration project from 1966 to 1968. The old structure was demolished, except for the façade and towers. The façade that remains features the coat of arms of Pope Pius XI, and many native plants are also in the design, including yucca and saguaro blossoms. The cathedral has seating for 1,250, and the floor is raked, so the main altar can be seen from the back of the Cathedral. The stained-glass windows were also restored.

Best Time to Visit: February to May

Pass/Permit/Fees: Free

Closest City or Town: Tucson

Physical Address: 192 S. Stone Ave., Tucson, AZ 85701

GPS Coordinates: 32.219294° N, 110.9714° W

Did You Know? The renovation cost over $1 million, which was donated.

Tucson Mountain Park

Tucson Mountain Park was created in 1929 by the Pima County Parks Commission, with C.B. Brown as chairman. Brown founded the park to help preserve the natural environment because of increasing development in the area. The park, which contains more than 20,000 acres, is one of the largest areas owned and operated by the U.S. Government. It is located within the Saguaro National Park and is used by hikers, equestrians, and mountain bikers.

There are 23 trails in the park, ranging from 1.6 to 13 miles in length. The Brown Mountain Trail is one of the most popular; it stretches 4.7 miles and is rated moderate. Hikers on the Bowen House and David Yetman Trails can view old, ruined houses. The Gilbert Ray campground is an excellent option for beginning campers. The Desert Discovery Center, on the western slope of the Tucson Mountains, offers stands of saguaro cacti and ironwood trees, along with spectacular views of the Altar Valley and surrounding mountains.

Best Time to Visit: March to May

Pass/Permit/Fees: Free

Closest City or Town: Tucson

Physical Address: Tucson Mountain Park, 8451 W McCain Loop, Tucson, AZ 85735

GPS Coordinates: 32.2133° N, 111.0862° W

Did You Know? Tucson Mountain Park has been the backdrop for many Western films.

Tumamoc Hill

Tumamoc is the O'odham word meaning "regal horned lizard." There is evidence that humans made their homes on the hill dating back 2,300 years ago. In the early 20th century, the hill became home to the Carnegie Institute's Desert Laboratory to study how plants survive in the intense heat and arid climates of the desert. The 860-acre ecological reserve is now a U.S. National Historic Landmark used for research and educational facilities, and the Steward Observatory has a small 20-inch telescope located on the hill. Many radio, television, and public safety transmitters are located on the top.

The Tumamoc Hill hike is a favorite among locals. The hike is 1.5 miles long and has a 700-foot rise in elevation. Some hikers simply go to the midpoint and back, while others aim for the summit. Benches are located along the trail, and a portable toilet and water fountain are available at the midpoint. During the spring months, wildflowers grow along with the trial and offer great photo opportunities.

Best Time to Visit: March to May

Pass/Permit/Fees: Free

Closest City or Town: Tucson

Physical Address: Tumamoc Hill Hiking Trail, Tumamoc Hill Rd, Tucson, AZ 85745

GPS Coordinates: 32.2255° N, 111.0016° W

Did You Know? The Desert Laboratory was founded in 1903.

Beaver Falls

Located on the Supai Reservation, Beaver Falls is on the trail to Havasupai and Mooney Falls. This waterfall is actually a series of smaller falls and pools created by sandstone and limestone. Similar to Havasupai Falls, calcium carbonate and magnesium cause the light blue color of the pool. The Havasu Creek runs through the falls and is a run-off from the Colorado River. A small dam was created on Havasu Creek to protect the falls and the pools because of the possibility of flooding during heavy rains.

Before 1910, these waterfalls were much higher, nearly 50 feet in some areas, but flooding destroyed many of the limestone ledges. There is no current in the water, making it excellent for swimming. Beaver Falls is a farther hike than Havasupai, making it an ideal location for a quieter escape. To see the falls requires an eight-mile round-trip hike from the designated trailhead at the campgrounds.

Best Time to Visit: April to June; September to October

Pass/Permit/Fees: 3-day permit needed, between $300-$400 per person

Closest City or Town: Tusayan

Physical Address: Havasupai Campground, Havasu Creek, Supai, AZ 86435

GPS Coordinates: 36.2825° N, 112.7294° W

Did You Know? A hiker in the 1970s threw his date seeds on the trail, so keep an eye out for a lone date palm tree after the third water crossing.

112

Grand Canyon

Arizona's Grand Canyon has been a place to visit for generations. Labeled as one of the Seven Natural Wonders of the World, it has an estimated 5.9 million visitors each year, making it the most popular national park in the United States. Carved out by the Colorado River over millions of years, the canyon is believed by some scientists to be nearly 70 million years old. Its unique rock formations and size can actually be seen from space. The deepest point of the canyon is 6,000 feet, and it is 18 miles across at the widest section. The canyon is so large that it contains five ecosystems: three types of forests and two types of desert systems. The deep canyons have allowed geologists to study and learn about the rock formations, offering a better understanding of the Earth and its history. Besides studying the rocks, anthropologists have been studying the remains of human villages found in the region.

Best Time to Visit: March to May; September to November

Pass/Permit/Fees: $35 Vehicle Permit (Day Pass) or $80 for an Annual National Park Pass

Closest City or Town: Tusayan

Physical Address: Grand Canyon Visitor Center, South Entrance Rd., Grand Canyon Village, AZ 86023

GPS Coordinates: 36.0591° N, 112.1903° W

Did You Know? Humans have lived in and around the Grand Canyon for over 10,500 years, since the last Ice Age.

Havasu Falls

Because of mineral deposits of calcium carbonate and magnesium, the Havasu Falls are naturally light blue. The bright color of the water and the contrast of the deep red hues of the sandstone rock have brought visitors to the region for years. But the trip to the falls requires a round-trip 10-mile hike. Havasu Falls is located in the Havasupai Reservation; "Havasu Pai" translates to "people of the blue-green water." In 1975, nearly 185,000 acres of land were returned to the Havasupai Nation.

The picturesque falls are known for the excellent swimming pool at the waterfall base. The water temperature stays at 70°F all year round due to the distance the Havasu Creek travels to reach the waterfall.

Best Time to Visit: April to May; September to October

Pass/Permit/Fees: 3-day permit needed, between $300-$400 per person

Closest City or Town: Tusayan

Physical Address: Havasupai Campground and Rangers Office, Havasu Falls Trail, Supai, AZ 86435

GPS Coordinates: 36.2552° N, 112.6979° W

Did You Know? The Havasu Creek passes through the Supai Village, one of the most isolated places in the United States. Helicopters deliver their food and supplies.

Ribbon Falls

Ribbon Falls is located in the Grand Canyon and is the only waterfall in the park that can be reached without backpacking or rafting. The falls are located along the North Kaibab Trail or the Phantom Ranch Trail, and the journey is about 12 to 16 miles round trip with an elevation change of 9,042 feet. The trek to reach Ribbon Falls can be very difficult for an amateur hiker. The falls are located 100 feet above the base of the pool and are full of rich minerals.

Ribbon Falls is a sacred site for the Zuni people, who believe this is where humans first emerged on Earth. Most people who hike to Ribbon Falls do it as part of a multi-day trip, given the intensity of the hike. The overhang of the cliffs around the falls offers a great place to rest from the sun during the summer. The water supply from the falls allows for lush vegetation compared to other areas of the Grand Canyon.

Best Time to Visit: March to May; September to October

Pass/Permit/Fees: Backcountry Camping Permit, $10 to $18 a day

Closest City or Town: Tusayan

Physical Address: Campgrounds near the falls are located at 20 N Kaibab Trail, North Rim, AZ 86052

GPS Coordinates: 36.1589° N, 112.0554° W

Did You Know? There is a massive green travertine spire underneath the falls from mineral deposits.

Chiricahua National Monument

Known as a "Wonderland of Rocks," the Chiricahua National Monument features rock spires standing among tall trees, offering a unique alternative to the typical Arizona landscape. These distinctive rock formations were given monument status in 1924 to protect the hoodoos and balance rocks. Hoodoos, or tent rocks, are tall, thin rock spires formed at the bottom of an arid drainage basin. The balancing rocks in the area are naturally occurring and are also known as precarious boulders.

The park includes Fort Bowie National Historic Site, the remains of a fort, and a cemetery created in the 1860s. A 17-mile trail system takes hikers around the park. Some trails will take you into canyons, while others will pass by rock spires. There are more accessible hikes for beginners and more strenuous ones for those with more experience.

Best Time to Visit: March to May; September to November

Pass/Permit/Fees: Free

Closest City or Town: Willcox, Arizona

Physical Address: Chiricahua National Monument Visitor Center, 12856 E Rhyolite Creek Rd, Willcox, AZ 85643

GPS Coordinates: 32.0136° N, 109.3423° W

Did You Know? There is a cabin in the park that was home to Swedish immigrants in 1887.

Raptor Ranch Birds of Prey Park Historic Bedrock City

This park features cute photo-ops, slides, swings, and life-size replicas of the Flintstones' home, school, hair salon, and other sets from the cartoon. The original park was built in the 1970s. Raptor Ranch Campground preserved the iconic Bedrock City in 2019 when it installed a brand-new birds of prey attraction that features live falconry classes, flight demos, and hands-on experiences for families. Campers enjoy free flight demos and visits to Bedrock City, and campsites are only 20 minutes from the Grand Canyon's South Rim.

RV and tent campsites are available, some with water and electric hook-up options, and there is free Wi-Fi at the campground. Water hookups are not available during the winter months.

Best Time to Visit: March to October

Pass/Permit/Fees: Free for campers, $8 for visitors

Closest City or Town: Williams

Physical Address: Flintstones Bedrock City, 101 US-180, Williams, AZ 86046

GPS Coordinates: 35.6531° N, 112.1423° W

Did You Know? The Bedrock City park is listed as closed on most websites because Raptor Ranch cannot legally advertise it as part of the Hanna-Barbara franchise.

Sycamore Falls

This extraordinary waterfall is located only 1.5 hours south of the Grand Canyon. Its area covers 1.6 million acres of land in the Kaibab National Forest. Many sites offer evidence of volcanic lava flows. The falls received their name from the vast number of sycamore trees in the park.

The Willow Falls run into a natural stone pool, dropping 70 feet, and dramatic basalt cliffs tower above. The canyon is the second largest in the red rock country of Arizona and is popular among locals. The main trail, Sycamore Rim Trail, is an 11-mile total loop with many lookout points. There are five entry points on the trail, and you can access the falls with a walk of only one or two miles – or you can walk the entire loop. The waterfall is seasonal; during a drought or deep in the winter, there won't be any falls. During the summer, the basaltic walls are popular for rock climbing and slacklining. The spring is one of the best times to visit the falls because melting snow will create the strongest water flow of the year.

Best Time to Visit: March to October

Pass/Permit/Fees: None

Closest City or Town: Williams

Physical Address: Sycamore Falls Trailhead, Fire Rd 109, Williams, AZ 86046

GPS Coordinates: 35.1387° N, 112.0256° W

Did You Know? The sun sets behind the falls and is one of the best times to take photos.

Hoover Dam

Located on the border of Arizona and Nevada, this arch-gravity dam is one of the most famous in the United States. Construction took place between 1931 and 1936 to harvest the Colorado River's energy, and the Lake Mead Reservoir was created as a result. The top of the dam towers 530 feet above Black Canyon and the Colorado River. Generators within the dam provide power and water utilities for Nevada, Arizona, and California. When the Hoover Dam was created, it was the largest dam in the world.

The town of Boulder City was created to house and support the 10,000 to 20,000 workers needed to complete the project. The massive arch bridge located in front of the Hoover Dam was the first concrete-steel arch bridge built in the United States and the widest concrete arch bridge in the Western Hemisphere. The region around the Hoover Dam is full of hiking trails through the geological wonders of the area.

Best Time to Visit: All year

Pass/Permit/Fees: Free to visit, but tours cost additional fees

Closest City or Town: Willow Beach

Physical Address: Hoover Dam Visitor Center, 81 Hoover Dam Access Rd, Boulder City, NV, 89005

GPS Coordinates: 36.0161° N, 114.7377° W

Did You Know? Construction of the dam required 4,360,000 cubic yards of concrete. This is enough to create a highway from San Francisco to New York.

Liberty Bell Arch

Located in the famed Lake Mead National Recreation Area, Liberty Bell Arch is named after the Liberty Bell in Philadelphia. Shaped over time by wind and water erosion, a bell-shaped hole was formed in the rocks. The trail to Liberty Bell is 5.1 miles round trip with an 800-feet elevation rise. The hike is considered strenuous and is closed during the summer months because of the heat. The hike to Liberty Bell Arch offers a glimpse of the history of the area, including cable-car ore from when the region was used for magnesium mining. The old mine's entrance is still visible, and hikers can enter and look around. Reaching the top of the trail will also offer views of Black Canyon Overlook and the Colorado River flowing through 1,000 feet below. Located near the Liberty Bell Arch Trail, another track leads to the natural hot springs; many people will come here to relax during their hike.

Best Time to Visit: October to March; the trail is not open during the summer months.

Pass/Permit/Fees: $25 per vehicle

Closest City or Town: Willow Beach

Physical Address: Kingman Wash Lake Mead National Recreation Free Camping is 1.5 miles north from the Liberty Bell Trailhead at Kingman Wash Access Rd, White Hills AZ, 86445

GPS Coordinates: 35.9749° N, 114.7242° W

Did You Know? North of the arch is the famed Hoover Dam.

120

Meteor Crater National Landmark

Nearly 50,000 years ago, a meteorite hit the earth with a force equivalent to 2.5 million tons of explosives, resulting in a crater with a diameter of 0.737 miles and a depth of 560 feet. This crater holds one of the best-preserved meteorites due to its young age and the dry climate. The crater was hardly explored until 1891 when Grove Gilbert, head of the United States Geological Survey, studied the region, and it was identified as the first meteor crater. To further preserve the inside of the crater, no solo hiking is allowed within it. Only guided tours are permitted. The crater has been given many names since its discovery, including "Coon Mountain," "Coon Butte," and "Crater Mountain." In 1967, after attempts to make the crater public, it was given National Natural Landmark designation. The land is not under government protection because it is privately owned. The site also features the Discovery Center and Space Museum that includes the Apollo 11 space capsule.

Best Time to Visit: March to November

Pass/Permit/Fees: Tours are $11 (ages 6 to 12), $20 (ages 13-59), $18 (ages 60+)

Closest City or Town: Winslow

Physical Address: Meteor Crater National Landmark, I-40, Exit 233, Winslow, AZ 86047

GPS Coordinates: 35.0280° N, 111.0222° W

Did You Know? The crater is privately owned by the Barringer family.

Salome Jug

Also known as Salome Canyon, the Salome Jug is located in the Sierra Ancha Mountains. The Salome Wilderness Area encompasses 18,530 acres in the Tonto National Forest. Evidence of previous residents, the prehistoric Salado Indians, can be seen throughout the park. The canyon has two sections: the Upper Salome Canyon and the lower canyon, "the Jug." These canyons form a natural water park with swimming and water rafting. Salome Creek runs through granite walls. The trail follows the creek and offers many opportunities to swim. One of the most famous trail regions is at the end of a 30-foot cliff where many brave hikers have jumped into the water. Hikers can slide down the rocks into pools of water because erosion has created a smooth surface. The best time to visit Salome Jug is during the spring season, when the water run-off is the strongest, although the water will be cold. This is a popular place to visit during the summer season and a great way to escape the intense Arizona summer heat.

Best Time to Visit: May to September

Pass/Permit/Fees: None

Closest City or Town: Young

Physical Address: Salome Wilderness Trailhead, A-Cross Rd, Tonto Basin, AZ 85553

GPS Coordinates: 33.7712° N, 111.1357° W

Did You Know? The trail to Salome Jug used to be a jeep run, a favorite among those enjoying off-road vehicles.

Proper Planning

With this guide, you are well on your way to properly planning a marvelous adventure. When you plan your travels, you should become familiar with the area, save any maps to your phone for access without internet, and bring plenty of water—especially during the summer months. Depending on which adventure you choose, you will also want to bring snacks or even a lunch. For younger children, you should do your research and find destinations that best suit your family's needs. You should also plan when and where to get gas, local lodgings, and food. We've done our best to group these destinations based on nearby towns and cities to help make planning easier.

Dangerous Wildlife

There are several dangerous animals and insects you may encounter while hiking. With a good dose of caution and awareness, you can explore safely. Here are steps you can take to keep yourself and your loved ones safe from dangerous flora and fauna while exploring:

- Keep to the established trails.
- Do not look under rocks, leaves, or sticks.
- Keep hands and feet out of small crawl spaces, bushes, covered areas, or crevices.
- Wear long sleeves and pants to keep arms and legs protected.
- Keep your distance should you encounter any dangerous wildlife or plants.

Limited Cell Service

Do not rely on cell service for navigation or emergencies. Always have a map with you and let someone know where you are and how long you intend to be gone, just in case.

First Aid Information

Always travel with a first aid kit in case of emergencies.

Here are items you should be certain to include in your primary first aid kit:

- Nitrile gloves
- Blister care products
- Band-Aids in multiple sizes and waterproof type
- Ace wrap and athletic tape
- Alcohol wipes and antibiotic ointment
- Irrigation syringe
- Tweezers, nail clippers, trauma shears, safety pins
- Small zip-lock bags containing contaminated trash

It is recommended to also keep a secondary first aid kit, especially when hiking, for more serious injuries or medical emergencies. Items in this should include:

- Blood clotting sponges
- Sterile gauze pads
- Trauma pads
- Second-skin/burn treatment
- Triangular bandages/sling
- Butterfly strips
- Tincture of benzoin

- Medications (ibuprofen, acetaminophen, antihistamine, aspirin, etc.)
- Thermometer
- CPR mask
- Wilderness medicine handbook
- Antivenin

There is much more to explore, but this is a great start.

For information on all national parks, visit https://www.nps.gov/index.htm .

This site will give you information on up-to-date entrance fees and how to purchase a park pass for unlimited access to national and state parks. This site will also introduce you to all of the trails at each park.

Always check before you travel to destinations to make sure there are no closures. Some hiking trails close when there is heavy rain or snow in the area and other parks close parts of their land for the migration of wildlife. Attractions may change their hours or temporarily shut down for various reasons. Check the websites for the most up-to-date information.